REFORM AND RENEWAL IN HIGHER EDUCATION

LIBRARY ORIENTATION SERIES

Number one: LIBRARY ORIENTATION; Papers Presented at the First Annual Conference on Library Orientation held at Eastern Michigan University, May 7, 1971.

Number two: A CHALLENGE FOR ACADEMIC LIBRARIES: HOW TO MOTIVATE STUDENTS TO USE THE LIBRARY; Papers Presented at the Second Annual Conference on Library Orientation for Academic Libraries, Eastern Michigan University, May 4-5, 1972.

Number three: PLANNING AND DEVELOPING A LIBRARY ORIENTATION PROGRAM; Proceedings of the Third Annual Conference on Library Orientation for Academic Libraries, Eastern Michigan University, May 3-4, 1973.

Number four: EVALUATING LIBRARY USE INSTRUCTION; Papers Presented at the University of Denver Conference on the Evaluation of Library Use Instruction, December 13-14, 1973.

Number five: ACADEMIC LIBRARY INSTRUCTION: OBJECTIVES, PROGRAMS, AND FACULTY INVOLVEMENT; Papers of the Fourth Annual Conference on Library Orientation for Academic Libraries, Eastern Michigan University, May 9-11, 1974.

Number six: FACULTY INVOLVEMENT IN LIBRARY INSTRUCTION: THEIR VIEWS ON PARTICIPATION IN AND SUPPORT OF ACADEMIC LIBRARY USE INSTRUCTION; Papers and Summaries from the Fifth Annual Conference on Library Orientation for Academic Libraries held at Eastern Michigan University, May 15-17, 1975.

Number seven: LIBRARY INSTRUCTION IN THE SEVENTIES: STATE OF THE ART; Papers Presented at the Sixth Annual Conference on Library Orientation for Academic Libraries held at Eastern Michigan University, May 13-14, 1976.

Number eight: PUTTING LIBRARY INSTRUCTION IN ITS PLACE: IN THE LIBRARY AND IN THE LIBRARY SCHOOL; Papers Presented at the Seventh Annual Conference on Library Orientation for Academic Libraries held at Eastern Michigan University, May 12-13, 1977.

Number nine: IMPROVING LIBRARY INSTRUCTION: HOW TO TEACH AND HOW TO EVALUATE; Papers Presented at the Eighth Annual Conference on Library Orientation for Academic Libraries held at Eastern Michigan University, May 4-5, 1978.

Number ten: REFORM AND RENEWAL IN HIGHER EDUCATION: IMPLICATIONS FOR LIBRARY INSTRUCTION; Papers Presented at the Ninth Annual Conference on Library Orientation for Academic Libraries held at Eastern Michigan University, May 3-4, 1979.

Number eleven: LIBRARY INSTRUCTION AND FACULTY DEVELOPMENT: GROWTH OPPORTUNITIES IN THE ACADEMIC COMMUNITY; Papers Presented at the Twenty-Third Midwest Academic Librarians' Conference held at Ball State University, May 1978.

REFORM AND RENEWAL IN HIGHER EDUCATION:

IMPLICATIONS FOR LIBRARY INSTRUCTION

Papers Presented at the Ninth Annual Conference
on Library Orientation for Academic Libraries
held at Eastern Michigan University, May 3-4, 1979

edited by
Carolyn A. Kirkendall
Director, Project LOEX
Center of Educational Resources
Eastern Michigan University

Published for the
Center of Educational Resources,
Eastern Michigan University
by
Pierian Press
ANN ARBOR, MICHIGAN
1980

Library of Congress Catalog Card No. 80-81485
ISBN 0-87650-124-2

Z
711.2
.L47X
no. 10

Copyright © 1980, The Pierian Press
All Rights Reserved

PIERIAN PRESS
P.O. Box 1808
Ann Arbor, Michigan 48106

Contents

Preface . . . . page vii
    Carolynn A. Kirkendall

Introduction to the Ninth Annual Conference . . . . page ix
    Fred Blum

The Core and the Library . . . . page 1
    Sheila K. Hart

The Community College Librarian As Catalyst for
    Curriculum Change . . . . page 9
    Katherine H. Jordan

Getting a Larger Slice of the Budget Pie
    for Library Instruction . . . . page 21
    Richard M. Dougherty

Instruction, Communication and the Faculty . . . . page 29
    Joann H. Lee

The Changing Roles and Expectations of Academic
    Librarians . . . . page 39
    A.P. Marshall

The Four R's: Implications for Library Services . . . . page 49
    Cleo Treadway and *Josephine Bradley*

Project LOEX Annual Report . . . . page 69
    Carolyn A. Kirkendall

Panel Discussion: Practical Suggestions for Implementation—
    Strategies for Promoting Library Instruction . . . . page 73
    Charles W. Brownson

    Curriculum and the Community College Library —
        Pre-flections on Meeting the Challenge . . . . page 89
        Ruth Foley

    Keeping in Step by Setting Pace . . . . page 93
        Ann Neville

Library Orientation and Instruction—1978 . . . . page 97
    Hannelore B. Rader

List of Participants . . . . page 119

Preface

Carolyn A. Kirkendall
Director, LOEX Clearinghouse Exchange
Center of Educational Resources
Eastern Michigan University

The Ninth Annual Conference on Library Orientation for Academic Libraries was held May 3 & 4, 1979 at Eastern Michigan University. For the sake of continuing unity, the term Library Orientation is still used in naming this annual program. However, for the past several years Conference themes have dealt with a wide and often sophisticated range of library user education topics.

As in the past, readers of Conference proceedings are reminded that the printed versions of spoken presentations will always vary in readability.

The title of the Ninth Annual Conference is Reform and Renewal in Higher Education: Implications for Library Instruction. In deciding on a general theme for this meeting, the current back-to-basics movement discussed in higher education, and how and if such a movement would affect our field, came to the forefront. Basic studies committees at various institutions had published new and often controversial goals, and talk of a 'core curriculum' abounded. Resultant investigation discovered that there was disagreement as to whether any sort of change in basic studies requirements would appreciably affect library instructional services, and thus a timely Conference topic was born.

This publication contains speeches in the order in which they were presented at the annual meeting, and reflects the opinions of practitioners, administrators, and a faculty member from a variety of institutions.

An annotated bibliography of related literature published during 1978 is appended, as is a listing of all Conference participants and speakers.

Formal presentations were separated by organized group discussions, and the LOEX Conference staff is, as always, grateful to librarians who gave of their time and expertise to coordinate these informal group meetings.

All Conference attendees are again also appreciative of the continuous support and generosity of the Pierian Press, who sponsor the annual party get-together at this Ypsilanti meeting. And, as always, the Conference coordinator is thankful for the invaluable assistance of the LOEX Secretary, Michelle Barnes, for her cooperation, and particularly to the talented McKenny Union staff here at EMU whose efficiency is responsible for consistently well-received arrangements.

Above all, this year, special appreciation goes to the major speakers, whose contributions follow.

INTRODUCTION TO THE NINTH ANNUAL CONFERENCE ON LIBRARY ORIENTATION

Fred Blum
Director, Center of Educational Resources
Eastern Michigan University

This is the fifth time I've had the pleasure of welcoming participants to the annual "Conference on Library Orientation for Academic Libraries."

Once again almost 150 librarians and library science students from 26 states and Canada are registered. Most of you are from college and university libraries, but an increasing number, about 10% this year, are from community colleges.

In welcoming you today, I'd like to stress that you who are involved in library use instruction are in the forefront of current educational and library trends.

You may not have thought much about it, but you are leaders in continuing and life-long education, for what do you do when you teach someone to use libraries if not provide them with the chief tool for life-long learning?

You are leaders in career education, for where is someone better able to develop in his or her career than in the library?

You are leaders in inter-disciplinary education, for where are the disciplines better integrated than in our great libraries?

You are leaders in competency-based education, for those whom you teach must demonstrate specific competencies in the library.

You are involved in educational technology, for what else are the audiovisual and computer tools you use?

You are in the forefront of educational change, for where is change more rapid than in today's library?

You are among the most service-oriented, for you help patrons make better use of library resources.

And you are leaders in the teaching profession, for what aim is more worthy of the teacher than teaching students the art of learning on their own?

So I welcome you enthusiastically. Enjoy yourselves while you're here. And if you have time, between the panels and the parties, come visit us in the library. We'll be glad to show you around.

Have a good conference!

THE CORE AND THE LIBRARY

Sheila K. Hart
Acting Head of Public Services
Harvard College — Widener Library

In 1974 Henry Rosovsky, Dean of the Faculty of Arts and Sciences, called for a "major review of the goals and strategies of undergraduate education at Harvard." This was to lay the groundwork for the first significant revision of the undergraduate curriculum in thirty years. The current system of general education requirements was established in 1945 as a result of the report *General Education in a Free Society*. This document (which came to be known as the Redbook) set forth the philosophical principles and organizational patterns which came to dominate much of American higher education until the relaxation and abolishment of distribution requirements in the 1960's. At Harvard even though the basic division requirements were still in effect in the mid-70's, there was general agreement that the proliferation of courses had eroded the purpose of "Gen Ed." In addition the world and the state of knowledge that had shaped the Redbook had changed radically since 1945. The skills and knowledge which had defined a liberal education in the post World War II era seemed hopelessly outdated by the 1970's.

The proposal for a core curriculum sought to answer the question, "What does our Faculty and our university mean when we welcome a student at graduation to the company of educated men and women?" In 1977 the Task Force on the Core Curriculum emphasized the value of a core curriculum embodying the "knowledge, skills, and habits of thought that the Faculty considers to be of general and lasting intellectual significance." In May 1977 the Faculty voted overwhelming endorsement of the principles of nonconcentration course requirement and asked Dean Rosovsky to develop detailed recommendations and guidelines for a core curriculum.

In the Report on the Core Curriculum issued in early 1978 the underlying principles of a Harvard standard in undergraduate education that meets the needs of the late twentieth century are elaborated:

1. An educated person must be able to think and write clearly and effectively.
2. An educated person should have a critical appreciation of the ways in which we gain and apply knowledge and understanding of the universe, of society, and of ourselves. Specifically, he or she should have an informed acquaintance with the aesthetic and intellectual experience of literature and the arts; with history as a mode of understanding present problems and the processes of human affairs; with the concepts and analytic techniques of modern social science; with philosophical analysis, especially as it relates to the moral dilemmas of modern men and women; and with the mathematical and experimental methods of the physical and biological sciences.
3. An educated American, in the last third of this century, cannot be parochial in the sense of being ignorant of other cultures and other times. It is no longer possible to conduct our lives without reference to the wider world within which we live. A crucial difference between the educated and the uneducated is the extent to which one's life experience is viewed in wider contexts.
4. Finally, an educated individual should have achieved depth in some field of knowledge. Cumulative learning is an effective way to develop a student's powers of reasoning and analysis and for our undergraduates this is the principal role of concentrations.

The underlying conception of the Core Curriculum is a minimum acceptable standard of undergraduate education focusing on five key areas of intellectual discourse. As the report states, it is an "amalgam of diverse intellectual approaches, major substantive areas of knowledge and important basic skills." It differs from existing distribution requirements in that the categories of general education have been altered to reflect shifts in fields of knowledge and in approach to learning. Also built into the core curriculum proposal is a mechanism for the creation of new courses specifically designed or adapted to meet its needs.

Early in 1978 the Committee on the Core Curriculum presented detailed recommendations for a nonconcentration requirement in each of five areas. A Literature and Arts requirement will acquaint students with important literary and artistic achievements and will foster a critical understanding of how man gives artistic expression to his experience of the world. A History requirement will orient students historically to some of the major concerns of the contemporary world, and help them acquire some measure of perspective on the complexity of human interaction in specific situations in the past. A requirement in Social and Philosophical Analysis will introduce the central concepts and ideas of the social sciences and moral and political philosophy and will develop students' analytical skills in understanding the fundamental social institutions and concerns of contemporary society. A Science and Mathematics requirement will convey a general understanding of science as a way of looking at man in the world. Finally a requirement in Foreign Languages and Culture will expand the student's range of cultural experience and provide fresh perspective on his or her own cultural assumptions and traditions. In addition to these five areas, the report also outlined degree requirements in Expository Writing, mathematics, and foreign languages.

While these major changes were being planned for the curriculum we in the library had started to deal with our own quite different issues. Library instruction under its earlier guises had emerged. Tours became more bibliographically oriented, reference interviews became longer and more didactic, and by 1977 many of us at Harvard had started our own programs, scattered, eclectic and independent for the most part of administrative assistance and support.

The Establishment of the Subcommittee

In November 1977 a group of librarians at Harvard decided to request that a committee be formed to deal with instruction in library use. There were three important reasons why we sought the attention of the University Library Council on the issue of reader instruction for library use. First, we were concerned about the increasing complexity of bibliographic tools, especially card catalogs and interactive data bases. Second, we were aware of the growing interest among faculty and deans in the fuller exploitation of all the resources of the University, including library collections. Third, we were dismayed witnesses to the enormous lack of bibliographic sophistication among readers who should now be acquiring life-long skills in the use of libraries.

These factors pressed us to ask for ULC recognition of reader instruction as a desirable and integral part of library service at Harvard. The most effective form of recognition the ULC could provide would be to establish a ULC Readers' Services Committee Standing Subcommittee on Instruction in Library Use. This would constitute a gesture of support from senior librarians which is necessary to ensure that reader instruction will eventually be recognized in the wider University community as a fundamental aspect of the educational process. In the library system staff worked separately and in isolation to develop instructional programs, the need for which was evident; the Council's willingness to institutionalize its interest in these services would focus the attention of deans and faculty on our work, the effect of which was often negated by the lack of University-wide awareness of the kind of instructional service we are able to provide. In view of the long-range objective outlined above, we anticipated that a ULC Standing Subcommittee would undertake the following:

1. To survey the state of instructional programs in the Harvard University Library, including a review of staff perceptions of readers' needs which presently go untended. This survey will contribute to a calendar of instructional programs and events; it will form the basis of a published guide to instructional programs; it will supply the data from which to shape policy statements on instruction in library use in the future.
2. To provide co-ordination for instructional activities in the future, so that library users and staff as well are able to sense the inter-relatedness of library collections and services.
3. To foster an HUL institutional membership in the LOEX organization, so that the HUL will have access to the widely circulated instructional materials which LOEX provides. The Standing Subcommittee will determine the mechanism for distributing these to HUL staff, or for announcing their receipt.
4. To address other issues pertinent to reader instruction, such as the desirability of staff development programs and extramural cooperative activities.

We appended copies of the *ARL Management Supplement* of September 1977, which treats this subject comprehensively, as background material in support of our request.

The University Library Council approved our proposal and our first act was to survey the work already being done at Harvard. We were pleasantly surprised at the variety of programs already underway. The Subcommittee quickly planned two workshops. The first was by Harvard Librarians for Harvard Librarians and featured presentations on teaching a course, slide-tapes, giving workshops, the making of bibliographies, graphics in the library, audiocassette tapes and general tours. The second workshop was chosen by general request and dealt with graphics. Then by late 1978 we were confronted with the necessity of finding the best way of involving the undergraduate libraries with the implementation of the core curriculum.

Library Instruction for the Undergraduate

There are three major undergraduate libraries at Harvard: The

Hilles and Lamont Libraries for general studies and the Cabot Science Library which covers the physical sciences.

Our objective for instruction at Cabot, Hilles, and Lamont has been to have students make efficient use of library resources and library staff in obtaining information. Specifically, we want students to understand the function of the card catalog(s) and basic reference sources and their place in a typical search strategy. Instruction is currently rooted in the principle that users are more receptive to library instruction if it is based on an immediate need.

Our efforts for the last year and a half have been directed toward identifying those needs and discovering appropriate and efficient means of satisfying them. We know from our meetings with students at the reference desk that their knowledge of the library is often limited and limiting, they are confused by the number and variety of Harvard libraries, they waste time consulting inappropriate sources, and they hesitate to ask the librarians for advice. Reasons for their hesitation may include embarrassment, confidence that their skills are sufficient, or even non-productive encounters with librarians in secondary schools where the library may have had more social or disciplinary than academic connotations. So we try to make the atmosphere and attitude in the library conducive to free inquiry. The "Interruptions Welcome" sign on one of the reference desks has gone a long way in breaking the ice with students.

Present Status

Our first approach to library instruction was incorporated into orientation programs given for new students at the beginning of term. In Cabot, for instance, orientation is accomplished by means of a "slide tour" which includes instruction on the use of the Union Catalog, the local catalog, and *Current Journals in the Sciences* (CJIS). One to two hour sessions (independent of specific courses but taking advantage of faculty willingness to encourage attendance) have also been given on the following topics: the literature of the life sciences, the literature of the physical sciences, *Biological Abstracts, Science Citation Index* and resources for environmental studies.

Hilles and Lamont Libraries initiated general workshops in the fall of 1977. Of the sixty students who signed up last fall, thirty-eight attended. From student evaluations we learned that the greater part of the information provided was new to the majority of them, and the most helpful aspects of the workshop, they said, were the introduction to previously unfamiliar sources such as indexes to periodicals, statistics sources, and the like. We found that the advantage of offering general workshops is that those who attend are highly motivated and have already acknowledged the value of knowing about libraries, also that group instruction is certainly the most efficient method for librarians to provide information of general value. Some of the drawbacks of general workshops are that we cannot require attendance and, although we know students' efficiency in use of library resources increases, we cannot measure how that improved efficiency is reflected in their work.

Expository Writing and the Undergraduate Libraries

Now to the Expos Connection.

Expository Writing is not a new Harvard institution, but its importance has been dramatically emphasized in the Core Curriculum plans. Expos, as it is called, is the one unavoidable requirement for all Harvard undergraduates. Consisting of a variety of subject-related half-courses, it aims both to teach the scientist to communicate with his readers and the English major to analyze his text with elegance; in short, Expos has as its goal the teaching of students how to write, a very basic skill to which the Core Curriculum accords the utmost importance.

Meanwhile back in the library . . . .

Although we have provided course-related instruction since 1975, our association with Expository Writing began in the fall of 1977, opening up for the first time the opportunity of reaching every student in the College. In the beginning, the sessions with Expos were based on the general workshop format with some modifications depending on the class. Later in the semester we determined that subject specific workshops could and should be offered to classes requesting them, with the stipulation that at least one week's notice be given to permit us time to research and obtain the necessary information, samples, slides, etc. In the fall of 1978 we met with twelve different Expository Writing sections (English and Social Studies) and one Freshman Seminar, a total of 207 students attended. Each of the sessions was custom designed and students were given a variety of handouts based on a previously assigned topic, and a fairly standard procedure was followed.

Class sessions usually begin with a discussion of the relationships among Harvard Libraries and what is to be found in each. The Union Catalog is explained. We raise some or all of the following questions and suggest ways of answering them:
    1. If you have a topic and want to find out what materials are available on it in Lamont (or Hilles, or Widener . . .), where do you start?
    [Discussion of the card catalog(s), what it does and does not

contain, and what subject headings to use in researching the assigned topic.]
2. If you need very recent information or if your topic doesn't lend itself to book length treatment, how do you go about finding periodical articles?
[Discussion of the differences among periodical indexes, how and why to use them.]
3. Will you need to find factual information, statistics, definitions, biographies?
[Discussion of the appropriate reference sources, with examples brought to the classroom, and explanations of their use.] We normally list alternative sources which perform the same function so that one title will not be in unnecessarily heavy demand.

We stress the role of the reference librarian, who should be used as one would a professional in any field, as guide, philosopher and friend.

Some of the advantages in offering the Expository Writing class sessions vs. general workshops are as follows:
1. The most important of all. We have the potential to reach every undergraduate in the College at a most vulnerable and formative part of his or her career, introducing them to the library as a primary and integral part of the Harvard experience.
2. Students are receptive to the presentation because it relates to an immediate need – the completion of an assigned paper.
3. Attendance is assured because it is a regular class session. Experience has shown that nearly all of the students attend these library class periods.
4. Students are sensitive to an instructor's use of class time. They are in a position to witness the value an instructor places on obtaining sufficient and accurate information, and on the role librarians can play in helping students use their time most efficiently and profitably.
5. We have a better opportunity for evaluating the success of library instruction through the observations of the Expository Writing staff.

Concomitant with all this, in 1978 a new and exciting program was started for sections of Expository Writing connected with the sciences. Scientist-authors, librarians and teachers of Expos combined forces to present their own special contributions to the production of published research results. Authors spoke of the importance of assuring accuracy while at the same time increasing accessibility to the information, and casting it into a form which will encourage reading enjoyment. The librarians' role has been to describe methods of gaining access to information needed, developing search strategies, and methods of checking and verifying the information available. The attractiveness of the program is in the presentation of these various components in a forum with students whose responsibilities require the understanding, use and to some degree emulation of each of the three specialties.

Postscript

In this short paper I have confined myself to an overview of the history of the Core Curriculum, the Instruction in Library Use program and the beginnings of intimacy between the two.

Of the future impact of the "Core" on the library, we can only speculate. An estimated sixty new courses are projected for the next few years. Only the increased emphasis on music has been already felt, with our music listening facilities having to be upgraded and numerically increased as soon as possible.

As of this writing, April 1979, the new course descriptions have not yet been announced, although rumour hath it, many are complete. Our plans for the immediate future are still in the making. The Expos connection will be further exploited, and plans for the calendar as outlined earlier, are underway. In Widener, we are hoping to start faculty seminars along the Berkeley line in the fall of 1979. The enthusiasm for library instruction at Harvard is growing and we have much to look forward to in the years to come.

THE COMMUNITY COLLEGE LIBRARIAN
AS CATALYST FOR CURRICULUM CHANGE

Katherine H. Jordan
Head, Instructional Services
Northern Virginia Community College
Alexandria Campus Library

Just as many four-year institutions begin to flex their leadership muscles and undertake the rigorous planning that will give new direction to their general education programs, so, too, are there signs of change, of renewal, in spite of the community college's long search for clarity or purpose. Let me briefly identify some reasons why community colleges will be latecomers to the process of general education renewal.

First, there is the breadth of the community colleges' mission, which almost makes impossible a single clear focus for its curriculum. The mission of the comprehensive community college requires it to provide academic programs to meet the needs of transfer students, occupational students, and general education students in addition to providing programs of remediation, a range of student services, and a responsive program of continuing education and community service. It has not been easy to be all things to all people.

A second factor which compounds the search for clarity of curricular purpose is essentially a funding problem. On the one hand, federal monies -- particulary in the form of Basic Educational Opportunity Grants to disadvantaged students -- have swelled enrollments of non-traditional students requiring basic skills instruction. Between 1954 and 1974, financial aid to students increased 6,000 percent (Cross, 1976). But paralleling this trend has been steadily decreasing state and local support for the community college budget as these jurisdictions reset their funding priorities -- especially in the wake of Jarvis-Gann, and this is reducing the ability of the community college to give much attention to the needs of its general education and transfer students.

A third trend is evident in the thinking of some educators who propose a new focus, a new identity for the community college. Calling for an expansion of the community college's mission to its community, these educators suggest that the community college will and should serve as an academic switchboard for all the community's diverse needs and programs. Proponents of the so called "community-based" model point out that growing numbers of adult and part-time learners in our communities seek to enhance the quality of their lives through varied educational experiences. The role of the "community-based" community college is one of facilitating the planning, structuring and delivery of educational services in the community (Myran, p.5).

Interestingly, it has been in the face of these trends and issues that Miami-Dade Community College has turned -- or returned -- to a redefinition of its mission and goals in terms of its general education program. Nearly three years in the planning, Miami-Dade's program, "General Education in a Changing Society" encompasses a core curriculum, a basic skills requirement and standards of academic progress.

Another indicator of interest in revitalizing general education is the very recently established Project on General Education Models. With funding from Exxon Educational Foundation and the Fund for the Improvement of Postsecondary Education, this three-year project has been established to create a consortium of 14 diverse institutions each of which will conduct a review of its general education program. Although only two of the 14 institutions are community colleges, it is clear that the Project and the models that result will be closely scrutinized by all kinds of institutions.

It is my contention that the 1980's will bring widespread curriculum renewal which will update and reaffirm the value of general education among community colleges nationally. I believe that the community college, in aligning itself with the values and purposes of general education for *all* its students -- not just those in its transfer programs -- will not only overcome its problems of self-definition but will also ensure its place and importance as an institution of higher education.

Although I want to further explore a new definition of general education for the 1980's in the first part of my remarks today, the meat of my message has to do with the role of the academic librarian -- and particularly the community college librarian -- in the process of curriculum change in our institutions. My message is that teaching librarians, or instructional librarians, have a rare opportunity to not only participate in curriculum renewal, but also to help chart its course. I am proposing a role that is bolder and more challenging than what we have typically defined as an adjunctive and an entirely service-oriented one; it would position us at center stage, rather than in the wings. And if that is where we decide we want to be, it behooves us to not only learn our lines, but to understand well the import of the drama. It means understanding the political and economic constraints operative in our academic milieu nationally and at our particular institutions; it means calling into question basic assumptions about the purposes and values of higher education, and it requires our involving ourselves in processes and activities on our campuses that will demand knowledge and leadership. It may mean our re-education!

This, then, is the challenge. I will return to the teaching librarian's role and give it a good deal more attention. First, however, I want to describe briefly the purposes of general education and suggest its present state of near demise at the community college. I also wish to offer a new definition of general education for the coming decade -- a definition which I think may give new direction to the meaning of lifelong learning and which expands upon the challenge I spoke of for the teaching librarian.

Before I do that, however, I had best explain why I chose to limit my remarks to general education rather than to the other major area of curriculum concern of the community college -- the occupational and technical programs. At the risk of appearing elitist in view of the enormous numbers of community college students enrolled in occupational programs -- nationally between 50 and 60 percent -- I would point out that education for specialization also requires a general education component (often pegged at about 25 percent of total credit hours) which is acknowledged to offer the critical conceptual and thinking skills that make the difference between educating for work and educating for a job. Ask the older and part time students who are returning to our campuses in ever greater numbers. They are the ones who realize perhaps more than the educators, how critical today is the need for knowing basic principles and concepts rather than narrowly defined skills -- for to have that knowledge base and the flexibility it gives one can make the difference between obsolescence and advancement.

Let us, then, consider the intent of a general education. Its purposes might be summarized as: (1) acquainting students with the ideas and theories of the disciplines; (2) nurturing those thinking and analytical skills that form the basis of lifelong learning; (3) offering an exposure to values, concepts and beliefs that provide a basis of personal growth, self-understanding and of contribution to one's society.

In 1977, the Carnegie Foundation for the Advancement of Teaching pronounced general education "an idea in distress." The reasons are not hard to find. Some of them date back to the increase in professionalization, the rise of the academic disciplines and the corresponding proliferation of academic departments and rivalries. As campuses across the country responded with "relevant" curricula to the demands of student activists of the sixties, all but the vestiges of organized curricular sequences leading to an acquaintance with the major ideas and theories of the disciplines were abandoned. Responding to the cultural relativism of the sixties, colleges and universities eschewed an education in values for value-free education (Cohen, p.4) -- and an education that would prepare students to think critically, to make choices, and to act upon their judgments. And so, with the exception of a few institutions, general education in the 1970's has floundered without direction, without leadership.

If general education was adrift in the four year institutions, it was all but lost at sea in the community colleges. Only the gross outlines of a general education program remain at the community college level, where integrated models of instruction have given way to free electives and distribution requirements.

Quite typical of the general education requirements for graduation from the community college is a program with a required sequence in English grammar and composition, a requirement in physical education and an orientation course; often no natural science or math requirement is stated. The remaining credit hours are to be chosen in a cafeteria style offering of electives. For example, additional humanities credits may be fulfilled with music, art, drama, languages, philosophy, speech or English. A rationale is provided: the student who has not yet set his or her academic goals can most profit by enjoying the flexibility which such an unstructured educational program can offer. To me, this is somewhat akin to providing a small child with a tray and unlimited access to all the food in the cafeteria. The adult abdicates any responsibility and the child has the fun of choosing any number of cakes and pies and sodas -- a sugar trip more than a meal.

While a great many of the community college students I come in contact with are already educated and are sophisticated about their goals for community college study, the great majority are especially needful of help at many stages of planning their academic programs; we do a great disservice by abandoning them to the educational cafeteria line.

The acceleration of change, the depersonalization of our institutions, the complexity of the world's problems and the urgency of our task demands nothing else than a reorientation of our thinking about general education, if our colleges are to provide students with the skills to participate in the solution-finding. And so, instead of relying solely on the time-honored tradition of general education, I propose that we consider "Education for Survival" as the appropriate educational mission of the 1980's. An "Education for Survival" would provide a curriculum organized on a thematic and interdisciplinary basis, linking scholarship to contemporary problems, it would rely on self-direction, upon an inductive mode; by providing a supportive learning environment, it would seek to nourish personal growth and a maturing ability to take responsible positions on the global issues of our time; finally, it would rely on a team approach for the delivery of instruction, requiring organizational patterns that bring together instructors, teaching librarians and counselors in a true community of scholars.

Today's students want and deserve the power to change things and the freedom that comes with knowledge, the understanding of self and the part that one can play in society. The students I work with choose research topics on the cost benefits of solar heating, the hospice movement, test-tube babies, international terrorism, the failure of the "green revolution." There is an eagerness to grapple with the big issues, and for a librarian it is exciting to share in the student's quest for information and meaning. Much of what goes on in the classroom, by contrast, often seems a bit lifeless and parochial.

To my mind, there is a bottom line to "Education for Survival" and it has to do with the skills to access and to use information. In his book, *Future Shock*, Alvin Toffler quotes psychologist Herbert Gerjuoy, "The new education must teach the individual how to classify and reclassify information, how to evaluate its veracity, how to change categories when necessary, how to move from the concrete to the abstract and back, how to look at problems from a new direction -- how to teach himself. Tomorrow's illiterate will not be the man who can't read; he will be the man who has not learned how to learn" (p.414).

What better description of an instructional librarian than one who teaches people how to learn? But by teaching people how to learn, I don't mean teaching particular techniques of ordering Library Congress numbers or explaining the minutiae of the collation -- though these may well be important things for a student to know. But if tomorrow's students are to make some contribution to our planet's survival, we must make available to them a correspondingly holistic view of learning resources. And if general education and "Education for Survival" suggest to you as they do to me a grounding in the conceptual structures, the great ideas and the modes of inquiry common to the disciplines, then the learning resources center, or the library, is the model that most closely corresponds to a general education; and if inductive modes of inquiry are encouraged and if independent and self-directed learning are nurtured in this new educational environment, does not the learning resources center serve as the laboratory for this new "Education for Survival?"

The challenges for the teaching librarian are implicit in such a model. To accept the challenge would mean that the teaching librarian would need to align himself or herself with the teaching-learning process, to view our role as essentially teachers, not technicians. By this, I don't mean to minimize the critical technical functions of the library, but only to underscore that how we view ourselves will have considerable impact upon our level of participation in the process of curriculum change.

Let me particularize and offer some notions about the forms which such a realignment of our role and purpose might take. Much has been said in the literature of library instruction about gaining support for the teaching library concept among teaching faculty and administrators. In community colleges today, deans and provosts have their hands full shoring up enrollments, competing for dwindling funds, dancing to the tune of ever more state control over instruction, and generally finding creative ways of doing more with less. We might deduce that instruction in the use of libraries is not going to capture the imagination of your typical administrator. Unless, that is, the teaching library is smart enough to align its mission and goals with those of the institution. The University of Wisconsin at Parkside is a case in point. Under Chancellor Alan Guskin's leadership, Parkside's mission was defined as providing academic programs and leadership in a responsive, community-based curriculum. Correspondingly, the library, under Joe Boissé's leadership, undertook greater collaboration with the public schools, public libraries and other community agencies, in addition to their already extensive campus-based programs of library instruction. Among the elements that affected the course of the teaching library at Wisconsin-Parkside, according to Guskin, was understanding how administrators operate:

> Since senior university administrators spend a good part of their week dealing with requests for funds, they become cynical about the importance of new programs that are add-ons to present programs. They are easily surprised and their imaginations stimulated when someone does *not* ask them for anything but rather shows them a new and exciting idea for increasing the effectiveness of a library by teaching students how to use it properly. Since libraries are generally seen as mausoleums where books are accumulated, as being a "bottomless pit" for monies to increase the collection, and as being passive recipients of a student population with decreasing skills, administrators may well be pleased by, and attracted to, an aggressive library that is teaching oriented, that doesn't want huge amounts of money, and that is educating students that need to upgrade their skills (p.11).

The Chancellor saw in the library a concrete and powerful endorsement of the campus philosophy, and thus, when the Chancellor, the chairman of the faculty and another faculty member sat down to develop a basic university skills requirement, someone suggested that research skills be added to those of reading, writing, and math. There was immediate recognition that Parkside's unique library skills program would fit their conception of a research skills requirement (Guskin, p.14).

Unlike the academic disciplines and divisions the library stands in a unique position in the academic structure to objectify and give substance to the institution's goals and objectives. And good things will come to those libraries who do.

Among the teaching faculty, I would see our main task as fostering an awareness of our interest in and knowledge of the teaching-learning process. Reference librarians at the College of DuPage spend a portion of each day in academic divisions, serving in a liaison capacity. What better opportunity to talk with faculty about the uses their students might make of learning resources?

At the Alexandria Campus of Northern Virginia Community College, we have used a campus-developed instructional development model for working with teaching faculty to build discipline-based, self-instructional programs in library use. The system is one in which proposals go through a planned sequence of development, review, evaluation and reporting. In our instance, the use of this plan has made possible faculty release time from teaching to work with us to develop instructional materials, has given us the benefit of advice and concrete improvements by a campus review team, and has provided visibility and credibility to our efforts among other faculty and administrators. It might interest you to know that the campus model calls for an LRC representative to sit on review teams of all instructional development projects.

There are other formal and informal ways of achieving a recognized campus role for librarians as educational leaders. In some institutions, librarians serve on curriculum committees and on committees that plan new courses. At Sangamon State University, this kind of participation has led to the initiation of some faculty and librarian team-taught courses. At my institution, we have invited instructors in various disciplines to bag lunch meetings with us. We encourage them to talk about their problems with library services and resources, about the ways their students are using the library, and we do some low key "show and tell" about some planned experiences in library use we have arranged for other departments and what those experiences have meant to the students. In the context of these bag lunch meetings, we have sought to carefully listen and respond to faculty concerns, and I believe our interest has been acknowledged. Two significant new library instruction activities have grown out of these sharing sessions -- as well as requests for doing them on a regular basis in the future.

Teaching librarians, if they are smooth and savvy enough, stand in a unique position to give classroom instructors thoughtful, informed and non-threatening feedback about the learning successes and problems of their students. Anyone who has been in on the building of a teaching library program knows how crucial it is to raise consciousness among our friends on the faculty about what the role of the teaching library is in instruction. You start where there is mutual trust and professional respect and build on that.

These, then, are some particular ways in which librarians can take a more assertive and more visible role in instruction. But in my judgment they are not enough if we are not up to date in our knowledge of the learning process. We can make some assertions that generally the more successful modes of instruction are experiential, individualized, provide immediate reinforcement, have clearly stated objectives -- but we also need to find out how to translate proven successful approaches into our own idiom. Carla Stoffle of the University of Wisconsin-Parkside, in a recent exchange of letters with a colleague, pointed out that instructional librarians need skills in teaching as do many other groups who are not primarily teachers -- social workers, extension agents, etc. Her proposal is that community education departments, or even library schools offer concise courses in adult learning, methods of teaching, and the use of media as an alternative to taking regular teacher education courses.

I have a final suggestion which also has to do with the updating of our own education. I suspect that nearly all of us have a background in general education along with our professional degree(s). For an undergraduate teaching librarian, I believe the most important credential is the strength of a general education. What else gives us the knowledge of the traditions of scholarship and the ability to give informed guidance to library users? Our library school education remains largely a technical one.

Knowledge, however, is not a static quotient; it grows exponentially. In contemporary society, problems are spawned faster than our ability to find answers. I propose another approach which has proven itself important to ourselves and our program -- that we enroll in courses on our own campuses. And not solely for updating our own education. In so doing, not only identify ourselves as lifelong learners; we also have the advantage of experiencing the education process from the student's point of view. Additionally, we will learn something about quality teaching from the good instructors, and we might end up serving as resource specialists in library-based learning at some future time.

These, then, are some particular notions about the librarian's role in the instructional process. We should recognize, however, that even a carefully articulated strategy which results in a closer realignment of the library with the teaching enterprise does not add up to the kind of educational leadership I spoke of earlier. To my mind the community college librarian can best play a catalytic role by embracing the goals of a renewed curriculum in general education which is available to all students.

If an "Education for Survival" is the task for the community college and if teaching librarians have a catalytic role to play in charting a new direction, they must acknowledge that an education for survival directly pertains to all the constituencies of the community college. I will briefly speak of three groups.

Some of the best general education today is going on in community based courses and forums. Problem-centered topics like the delivery of quality day care in the community, issues surrounding the location of nuclear power plants, represent the exciting exchange which survival education is all about. If a person is to deal with the issues of putting a power plant in his back yard, he will learn something about physics, the technical considerations of power plant design, the disposal of nuclear wastes and other environmental impacts, and he will examine his role in the political process – precisely the domain of general education.

Let us look at our older students -- the ones returning to our community colleges in large measure to upgrade their skills. They, more than any of our constituencies, are eager for the enrichment which general education can offer.

> They know that employment depends less on skill training than on the ability to get along with employers and co-workers. They know that a satisfying life demands more than production and consumption. They know they must understand the ways institutions and individuals interact, that for the sake of themselves and their progeny they must understand and act on social issues. They know . . . that what they learn assists them in maintaining individual freedom and dignity . . . And that is why they come to the colleges with interest in the arts, general concepts of science, relations with their fellows, questions of personal life crises and developmental stages -- all topics in a true general education curriculum (Cohen, p.23).

And what of our non-traditional, our disadvantaged students? They are the products of our public schools' failure to educate. For the most part they lack the skills to do college-level work. It has been estimated that one-third of the math now taught in the community college is 6th to 8th grade math and that half of the English taught is at the level of basic grammar. In response to the basic skills requirements of these students, a great deal of attention has been given to the provision of specially tailored educational programs and support services that will help ensure retention of these students. New instructional strategies such as mastery learning and Personalized Systems of Instruction are responses to the needs; cognitive mapping is being advocated as providing significant information about learning styles, thus permitting the individualizing of instruction.

What concerns me is the incredible need among these students for precisely those skills and experiences most common to general education offerings, and the possibilities for us as librarians for providing the information survival skills that might make a critical difference to the disadvantaged. Our new students are typically the information-poor of our society. They lack the basic knowledge of how human society is structured and the way it functions. And thus they do not know the ways in which information is packaged – in people, in print, in institutions, in the media. To find the name of a local government official, to get help from a landlord-tenant commission, to obtain a fishing license, to locate a public clinic -- all information access skills. They are the skills implicit in an "Education for Survival." To my way of thinking, community colleges are missing the boat by not offering general educational experiences to students in remedial programs. Our non-traditional students recognize their deficit; the day to day pressures they face may mean they will drop in and drop out of our colleges, but if they *know* that quality education will always be available to them in their community colleges, they will return. Arthur Cohen says, ". . . the community college either provides general education for all its enrollees or it forfeits its position in higher education" (p.29).

If the community college librarian is to be an agent of change, he or she must get busy and talk to faculty and administrators about a contemporary model of general education for all students. By all accounts, we live in a learning society; it has been estimated that the majority of American adults are involved in all manner of formal and informal learning activities both inside and outside of academic institutions. The ability to use the library's human and material resources are the very skills of lifelong learning, and the access to information by which we make informed choices will continue to be the source of our personal freedom.

REFERENCES

Carnegie Foundation for the Advancement of Teaching. *Missions of the college curriculum*. San Francisco: Jossey-Bass, 1977.

Cohen, A.M. *The case for general education in the community colleges*. Paper presented at the Forum on Future Purposes, Content and Formats for the General Education of Community College Students, Montgomery College, Maryland, May 22, 1978. (ERIC Document Reproduction Service No. ED 154 849.)

Cross, K.P. Beyond education for all -- toward education for each. *The College Board Review*, 1976, *99*, 5--12.

GEM Newsletter (Project on General Education Models), February 1979.

Lukenbill, J.D. and McCabe, R.H. *General education in a changing society; general education programs, basic skills requirements, standards of academic progress at Miami-Dade Community College*, Dubuque, Iowa: Kendall/Hunt Publishing Co., 1978.

Myran, G.A. Antecedents: evolution of the community-based college. *New Directions for Community Colleges*, 1978, *6*(1), 1--6.

Toffler, A. *Future shock*. New York: Bantam Books, 1970.

GETTING A LARGER SLICE OF THE BUDGET PIE FOR LIBRARY INSTRUCTION

Richard M. Dougherty
Director, University Libraries
The University of Michigan

I agreed to participate today, but only with some trepidation. My interest in bibliographic instruction is high but I questioned my qualifications to speak on the topic. I assume you are attending today in order to learn more about new developments and how to convince others of the value of bibliographic instruction. I certainly cannot hope to make you better classroom instructors, but possibly I can be of value by presenting to you a managerial perspective of bibliographic instruction, a perspective gained through a long tenure as a manager of libraries in academic settings.

A manager, even though committed to BI, is likely to view BI quite differently than many of you in the audience. Where your primary concern may be BI, it is one of many programs a manager must consider at budget time. You might believe that it is the manager's responsibility to create the climate for success, the manager might counter that creating the climate is a staff responsibility. One BI librarian explained the question of administrative commitment thusly:

> " . . . you must look at the extent of the administrator's commitment. Is he only paying lip service to an 'in' idea, or can he translate this idea into reality? Has the administrator clearly thought out the impact that such an undertaking will have on the system in terms of staffing patterns, cost for materials, clerical support and an increasing demand for more services of this type, a demand which will lead to pressures for hiring additional staff? Does the administrator realize that the time-frame required for the development of an extensive bibliographic instruction program will probably be measured in years, not months, and is he willing to invest the library's resources in such an untried, long-range plan?"[1]

I suggest that the reader substitute the word "staff" each time "administrator" appears, for in reality, the commitment to BI must be a combined staff/administrative venture, a commitment that can't be achieved without cost.

If one accepts the proposition that bibliographical instruction is a worthy activity, why haven't you been more successful in proselytizing others? Why haven't more faculty embraced the concept of bibliographic instruction? Why have so few of your library colleagues joined the cause? Why haven't library directors allocated a larger share of the budget to bibliographic instruction? These are all difficult questions to answer, but I plan to concentrate on the relationship of library directors to a BI program. I would like to go beyond the question of why directors do not allocate a larger share of the budget and also offer suggestions on how you might be more successful in your budget quest next year.

It is important that I establish the context in which we must all work. All of us must cope with increasing demands on our resources with budgets that are declining in purchasing power. In other words, we are being asked to do more with less. This situation is not unique to libraries. It is a plague visited upon the entire education establishment. We must also cope with the reality that people are less willing to accept change or to take risks when funds are scarce. This fact has been well-researched by social scientists. In effect, organizations are less likely to adopt innovative ideas during a time of budget scarcity. Now, I realize bibliographic instruction is not a new idea, but to a library that does not presently engage in formal bibliographic instruction, such a program does represent an innovation to *that* organization. Moreover, during a time of budgetary cutbacks, there is a tendency for organizations to trim services that are non-traditional. In other words, new or recently established services such as data base searching, bibliographic instruction, or campus document delivery services are most vulnerable to cutbacks.

We must keep in mind that bibliographic instruction is but one of a number of activities competing for library dollars. A library must continue to select, acquire, catalog, organize, circulate, and shelve many forms of materials; it must offer reference service, organize archives and manuscript collections, acquire and service AV materials, and operate reserve collections, to name but a few traditional library activities. When budget cuts occur, none of these activities are likely to be entirely eliminated. This is one of the special dilemmas that confronts the contemporary library manager. A budget cut mandated within an academic department may be localized, that is, untenured instructors offering specific courses can be given notice. But in a library, a cut is usually spread across-the-board simply because none of the basic library activities can be totally discontinued. For this reason, as I mentioned previously, it is the non-traditional activities that are most vulnerable to cuts during a period of retrenchment.

Let us assume for a moment that your program escapes budget reductions for the immediate future, and you have been successful in convincing colleagues and acquaintances on the faculty of the need for an expanded bibliographic instruction program. Four instructors, one each from the fields of education, forestry, history, and anthropology, have agreed to allow their students to participate in the library's instruction program and for the sake of our example, let us assume further that there are four staff members who are interested and who possess the qualifications to present the appropriate courses. The invitation sets into motion a period of intensive activity during which each library instructor strives to organize the appropriate materials into an effective presentation. Let us assume that courses, when presented, are well received. In fact, the professors indicate their intention to invite the librarians back the following year.

Now, what can we learn from the experience I've just desscribed? First, the content of the four courses was undoubtedly different, since the disciplines of education, history, forestry, and anthropology are not intellectually or bibliographically organized in the same manner, so that the course content would be be presented in the same way to the students. Second, the course preparation required an enormous amount of individual effort. In fact, it may have required a reshuffling of work schedules and in some cases it might have required supervisors to assign some regular duties to others on the staff. But all in all, the experience left a feeling of fulfillment because the library had demonstrated its ability to present material effectively, and it had shown there was a need for, a receptivity to information about the use of bibliographic tools.

In addition to the foregoing there are also some long-range implications that should be examined. The initial classroom success may stimulate new demands. Other instructors may seek out library services. If it worked for one instructor, why not another? Consequently, instead of having to serve four quite disparate disciplines one may have to consider offerings for English literature, chemistry, Germanic studies, etc. Does the library have the qualified staff? Is there adequate time for preparation? The answer to the first question is probably yes; that is, there are enough members of the staff who could present a respectable course. The answer to the second question may be no, there is not sufficient time for staff to prepare courses in light of other regular duties. In order for the library to assume the additional responsibility, the number of library instructors must be increased.

The scenario I have just described is the consequence of success breeding success. That is, one provides a service that stimulates new demands until the existing capacity to perform that service is saturated. It is at the point when current staff capacity becomes saturated that one may encounter resistance with a library director. A director may not appear to listen with a sympathetic ear. In the flush of success, the staff may not realize that it has been caught-up in what I call the "vicious cycle syndrome."

If there is an actual need for a service, and if the service capacity is expanded, additional demand for that service will be generated. This is a phenomenon very familiar to businessmen and government officials. In a sense it relates to the economic relationship of demand and supply. If the product creates a demand, the supply is likely to become limited. The scarcity drives prices up. As the price increases, the demand gradually diminishes: a classic example of the law of demand and supply. But in the non-profit sector, a product or service that creates a demand does not have the pricing mechanism to regulate demand and supply. Success only creates new demands. As one increases the capacity to perform a service, in other words as the supply is increased, the demand continues to increase in the absence of some pricing mechanism. This upward cycle would theoretically continue until all demands for the activity have been fully met.

The real problem is that we rarely achieve the condition of full saturation. Consider what is happening to the demand for interlibrary lending and borrowing activities and what could occur as data base searching becomes more popular. In both instances the demand for these services will continue to grow as our capacities to offer these services expand. In the case of interlibrary lending, especially with the advent of the OCLC interlibrary lending module it will become even easier to locate information about books; consequently, the demand for materials is likely to increase. The increased interlibrary lending traffic has already caused some libraries to impose sizeable borrowing fees, and if the trend is not reversed, other libraries are likely to impose fees, not to generate income, but to serve as a mechanism to control the level of demand. A similar demand/supply spiral could occur with the data base searching unless some sort of control mechanism is created. Knapp and Schmidt have some germane questions regarding pricing policy in their recent article.[2] This demand/supply spiral can create a vicious budgetary cycle for budget officers.

Our bibliographic instruction enthusiasts may have become victims of their own success. They reached the capacity of their existing resources. They can only satisfy additional demands by acquiring new staff resources.

So, I return to the basic question, how can one acquire additional resources at a time when the library's overall budget is not growing? In such a circumstance, a director must be willing to sacrifice other activities in order to accommodate additional bibliographic instruction activities. Faced with a static budget, the augmentation of any activity must be funded through the reallocation of existing funds. In order to achieve a fund reallocation, one or more of the following strategies may be adopted: (1) one or more activities be allowed to atrophy; (2) staff reductions achieved through normal attrition or through layoffs; (3) existing tasks performed more cheaply through the adoption of technology; or (4) existing tasks assigned to staff in a lower classification; or (5) funds diverted from the book and periodicals budget. There aren't too many other possibilities. I recognize I have offered what is tantamount to Hobson's choice, nevertheless, it represents what happens in the real world of budget preparation.

Another alternative is possible, that is, the library director can persuade the campus administration of the library's need for additional funds. And certainly directors must continuously and persuasively plead the library's case. But even though the effort is made, the prospects for success at most institutions do not appear bright. If a campus's budget is not growing, then the president or vice-president will have to engage in a similar process of budgetary reallocation. It will be no less painful at their level than it was for the library director. Something will have to be sacrificed in favor of bibliographic instruction. I am not suggesting that the effort should not be made, for of course, it must. What I am suggesting is that during the time of declining enrollments, a period of pernicious inflation, the chances for securing additional resources are not great, and one must keep expectation levels in rein.

What then is the best way for those interested in bibliographic instruction to expand their capacity during a time of budgetary decline, or stated simply, how do you get a larger share of the pie? In all libraries, large or small, this may depend most upon the level of your commitment to bibliographic instruction. How important do you rank instruction in relation to other activities performed by you and your colleagues? Are you willing to turn over some activities traditionally performed by professionals to the clerical staff? For example, are you willing to permit non-professional staff to answer directional or what is generally termed "ready reference" questions? Or are you likely to respond clerical staff or students can't do that unless they are supervised by a professional? I have heard this sentiment persuasively argued. On the other hand, I have read other equally persuasive studies that argue the opposite point of view. There is probably no entirely correct answer, but rather one must accept that there is a trade-off between increasing the time available to perform activities such as bibliographic instruction and the increased risk that library assistants will fail to provide the correct response to a ready reference question or will fail to perceive the real need of the user.

Similar trade-offs exist in other parts of the library. A particularly classic case can be cited from technical services. OCLC has expanded the typical library's capacity to catalog titles. It has made it possible for libraries to assign library assistants to perform tasks formerly performed by professional catalogers. But this process has not been achieved without its own set of choices onerous to some librarians. They are not willing to accept OCLC cataloging contributed by other institutions. If a title is not cataloged by the Library of Congress, then ideally it should be inspected by a member of the profession. I don't quarrel with the intent for I am sure the quality of cataloging occasionally can be improved through one additional inspection. But one should consider the economic consequences. Today in small and large libraries the cost of original cataloging may be two, three or even four times greater than the cost of cataloging when copy from either Library of Congress or OCLC is used. The argument of which is best is irrelevant today. I'm only suggesting that the resources available to perform non-traditional activities may be directly dependent on a staff's willingness to make choices, to take risks -- its willingness to adopt new approaches at the expense of traditional activities.

It has been my experience as an administrator, editor, and as an observer of the professional scene that library staffs too often are not willing to make these choices. Staff members are likely to react to the prospect of change in the same way as an acrophobiac views the edge of a deep precipice; that is they both take a quick glimpse, and then beat a hasty retreat into surroundings that are more familiar and more comfortable. This behavior pattern can be attributed to many library administrators as well.

I'm also often asked about the process of change and particularly the rate of change in libraries. To many observers, both initiated and uninitiated, the process of change in libraries appears to be so agonizingly slow. Paradoxically, if a library is managed in an autocratic manner, it is more the responsibility of the director to initiate action. Without the need to establish a staff consensus, change can appear to take place more swiftly. But if the library is managed in a more consultative, participatory manner, the staff must assume more responsibility to argue for and initiate actions that will lead to changes. In the latter model, there is a requirement for the entire staff to share in the risk taking and in the process of change. Change is likely to occur more slowly in libraries where there is widespread staff participation, but the changes that do occur are likely to achieve greater staff acceptance.

It is not too soon to begin planning for the next five years. Oftentimes, a lack of success can be attributed directly to the failure to develop a plan. One must establish goals and objectives, outline a strategy of implementation, consider what resources are currently available, what additional resources can be expected in the near future, and if necessary, what activities will have to be adjusted in order to accommodate a new or expanded bibliographic instruction program. Keep in mind the need to reexamine your own priorities in developing a plan. If you and your colleagues accept choices and recommend changes such as those suggested earlier, this will strengthen the plan and enhance your persuasiveness in convincing directors that the plan should be funded.

Let me summarize some of what I believe to be the most important points. Generally bibliographic instruction has not swept the academic community because its value is not universally understood or accepted, and if universal acceptance were to be achieved, there would be inadequate resources to meet the greater demand. The current budgetary situation and the outlook for the near term do not augur well for additional resources. And, libraries are in danger of creating new demands for services at exactly the time its capacity to provide additional services is often over taxed. If library staffs can agree that bibliographic instruction, data base searching and other non-traditional activities are important, then it becomes incumbent upon a staff and its director to determine together how resources can be reallocated and what activities need to be trimmed in order to accommodate an expanded instruction program.

In spite of my seeming pessimism and caveats, I believe it is possible to obtain a larger share of your library's budget, so long as you and your colleagues and your director are willing to make the hard choices necessary to achieve the goal of expanded bibliographic instruction programs.

FOOTNOTES

1. Lossing, Sharon. "Reaching Graduate Students: Techniques and Administration." *Faculty Involvement in Library Instruction*; Papers and Summaries from the Fifth Annual Conference on Library Orientation for Academic Libraries. Ann Arbor: Pierian Press, 1976, p. 90.

2. Sara D. Knapp and C. James Schmidt, "Budgeting to provide computer-based reference services: a case study," *Journal of Academic Librarianship* 5:1 (March 1979) p. 9--13.

INSTRUCTION, COMMUNICATION AND THE FACULTY

Joann H. Lee
Head, Reader Services
Donnelley Library
Lake Forest College

As the theme of our conference indicates, reform is taking place in our academic institutions today. But what is the direction of this reform? Let me read you a few recent quotations from academic circles to see what you think.

"The problem... is the tendency .... to see education as a vast smorgasbord, where a student's tastes alone determine whether he or she will receive proper educational nutrition." Schiefelbein (p. 13).

"... Professors can easily fall into the habit of simply arranging a body of knowledge in a logical sequence ... to convey a wealth of factual material, generalizations, and ideas, embroidered by the instructor's own interpretations and insights .... Experienced teachers in many colleges tend to devote almost all of their undergraduate teaching to the process of conveying information and knowledge through lecturing to students. Much less attention is paid to the task of training students to think clearly and communicate with precision and style." Bok (p. 159, 161, 163–4).

"The great irony of the situation is that the impulse to reform spends itself ... in a single stereotypical way, namely, changes in curriculum." Bayley (p. 591).

These statements indicate that there is nothing static about the concerns of higher education nor is there much consistency about ideas for its reform. But change it will, and while the faculty are busy implementing the changes they have fought for ... or against ... it behooves us as librarians to become involved in these changes, while understanding all the possibilities.

Earlier you heard about reform and renewal at Harvard, Northern Virginia Community College, and the University of Michigan.

How do I fit in? My perspective is that of a librarian in a small liberal arts college, Lake Forest, where curriculum reform has taken place gradually. My contribution is to detail the experimentation we are conducting in planning library instruction and involving faculty in its implementation. Also, to save others from conducting the sometimes expensive research we've undertaken – a direct result of several grant-funded faculty development programs -- I'd like to spend some time describing these programs for you. First you'll need to know a bit more about how we operate.

At Lake Forest our low faculty/student ratio helps guarantee close contact between the two groups. In addition, as Margaret Mead has said, "a student (is one) who lives in college and whose degree depends upon his sleeping there." (p. 27). Not as silly as it sounds, this essentially captive position of students, typical of a small liberal arts college, has the effect of strengthening faculty/student relationships. Faculty are more perceptive of changing student needs. Furthermore, with a limited bureaucracy, and nearly autonomous faculty, reform can come more gradually than in either large universities or state supported institutions.

So at Lake Forest College it's inexorably back to the core or structured curriculum, a move which I feel will have a most salutory effect on library instruction. Under the open curriculum, librarians struggled for years with the task of providing individual instructional segments in an amorphous beginning level program, frequently without even a required ground work course in science or English composition. But now with the vast increase in the output of information resources and the further needs of faculty to impart this burgeoning body of information, librarians will assume an increasingly important role in aiding students to understand and work with these resources.

The key is in the word structured. A tighter organization imposed on the curriculum lends itself to better library instruction coverage. The limited number of courses on the basic level make it possible for us to reach all students with fewer unique preparations.

This curriculum revision is an indication also that faculty believe students build on basic structured courses in developing proficiency in a major. It will be easier to insist that students learn library use in small increments, too. Reason: if you can't learn biology in one course, neither can you learn library and research skills for biology in one session. Such skills develop along with subject knowledge, along with reasoning skills, along with understanding.

Our faculty were coming to grips with some of these needed reforms when the library became the recipient of two grants which gave us the opportunity to experiment with new methods of library instruction. At the same time two departments of the college were also awarded faculty development grants. One served to put impetus behind a many faceted program to develop students' writing skills, another introduced computer programming methods in a number of academic disciplines and classroom situations. The two library grants supported the involvement of faculty members in library instruction.

Just how did we tie in our activities with those of the faculty grant recipients as well as make use of the changes in curriculum that were taking place? How did we use communication with faculty and students to develop library instruction components in the freshman English courses, other beginning level courses in subject disciplines and advanced research courses in these disciplines?

Our first effort at faculty involvement in library instruction occurred at the pre-school conference, fall of 1977, at which the faculty were introduced to the writing skills program. This program, which includes English Composition, was an early target because by that time we had a de facto writing competence requirement and more and more sections of composition were being conducted every year, and each required four librarian-led instructional sessions.

We developed an experimental set of guides to introduce students to basic library tools and methods for these English Composition courses. Librarians participated in some classes but in others, the materials, along with a simple search strategy, were introduced by the teaching faculty. Needless to say, there were as many methods of implementation of the core program as there were instructors. But our evaluation showed that both students and faculty were satisfied with the results. At the end of the sessions, questionnaires filled out by 94 students indicated that they felt that they had learned library skills as much from faculty as librarians. Also, in individual interviews, we found that faculty were generally satisfied with student performances on the research assignment. So, involvement of faculty in library instruction paid off.

With the program, taught primarily by faculty, as an accepted element of students' writing skills instruction, we were able to attend far fewer sessions of freshman English than previously. Relinquishing this heavy commitment left us with more time to concentrate on the next area in need of library instruction, the subject discipline.

When faculty reduce the number of available courses in a subject and structure the remainder in a sequence, they make it easier for us to develop basic library instruction in the subject. We prepared a basic guide which could be adapted for elementary courses in a number of subjects. It was used to develop a class session in which students were active participants. They discussed search strategy, examined a preselected set of tools, evaluated the tools and described them to the class. Using this format, the librarian assures the involvement of students, but, in return, relinquishes a measure of control. Since she does not know the members of the class, she is never sure when she sticks her neck out what's going to happen to it. Sometimes there are negative or smart-alecky students who will challenge her. That is one of the chances she takes, but at least she can see a more direct response to the material and ideas she is introducing than in the lecture format.

If faculty, students and librarian all participate in an informal give and take it seems to provide students with a better sense of how to investigate for their own topics, and therefore to produce a better end product -- the research paper. After several terms in some of these classes, faculty have shown a willingness to conduct their own sessions based on the guides.

Another plus for the design of this guide is its flexibility and adaptability which make it usable in several disciplines. Preparation time for other classes is reduced.

Here, again, as in the composition program, when we found a way to reduce our work load, we could move into other areas of instruction.

The next logical step was to involve faculty in library instruction on the research level of an academic discipline. For this exalted level we felt that we needed to have an unusual approach. We began experimenting with an exciting new gimmick for library instruction, that of online periodical index data base searching.

"Humph," you say, "we've all heard of online searching, but what does it have to do with library instruction?"

"Well," as the patent medicine salesman would say, "ladies and gentlemen, I'm gonna tell you . . . "

You may just guess that I'm really a convert to computer searching and as my horse "Obie" would tell you, I'm *not* a machine-oriented person by nature. How many of you work in libraries which do data base searching? How many search? No? I think if you try it, you'll like it.

Online searching is an intriguing a puzzle as the best reference question because data bases vary from each other as much as other reference tools.

But let me explain how data base searching renews communication with faculty and how it fits into advanced library instruction. First, I'd like to use my experience at a *Chemical Abstracts* services training session at the Institute of Paper Chemistry as an example of how searching affects faculty. This session purported to explain to chemistry professors the use of *Chem Con*, the online version of *Chemical Abstracts*. I was accepted for attendance at the conference and joined the chairman of our chemistry department and a dozen other chemistry professors of assorted ages, sexes, and academic affiliations. I learned three important things.

First, but not necessarily most important, I learned a good deal about *Chem Abstracts*, both on- and off-line, and about the structure of chemical literature. Second, I absorbed some teaching techniques from a very well-organized presentation. And, third, I saw faculty members impressed with the need for communicating with their students concerning the literature of their field.

I listened to a group of interested chemistry teachers admit that they would never have come to a session which purported to tell them about changes in *Chem Abstracts*, but were drawn into the session by the idea of learning about a new "gimmick": data base searching. Then they freely confessed that they really hadn't known how to use the printed form of the abstracts to its best advantage either since so many changes had taken place since their student days.

Lake Forest's own professor representative, at least, returned to campus determined to do a more thorough job of training his students in the use of the literature. He now requires that they do sample literature searches he has developed from the material presented at the training session. He does all of his own instruction asking only that the librarian perform computer searches for term papers or senior theses and explain to students how articles located in a literature search are obtained.

As a result, instruction is better in chemistry, and communication is now greatly improved between faculty member and librarian -- not to mention students. This pattern of cooperation and more effective communication has been repeated whenever we introduce data base searching in a department.

Our Council on Library Resources Library Service Enhancement Project grant enabled us to develop a bibliographic instruction component with primary emphasis on data base searching that we have adapted for research courses in several subject disciplines. The plan was integrated into a new interdisciplinary seminar in the health services which served as an excellent experimental ground for determining the strengths and weaknesses of the scheme before it was revised for specific subject disciplines.

This course was created by a committee which represented six different academic departments. Our involvement in the Health Services Institute Seminar was assured by commitments made when we applied for our grant, but the success of the experiment was partly attributable to the support of the head of the economics department. He and I had worked together for many years to include library instruction in economics research courses. His influence on the other five faculty members involved in this interdisciplinary course was significant.

Our instructional package for the course was designed to help students become better equipped to use all methods of information retrieval and to understand the relationships among various types of sources. We avoided over-emphasis of the computer gadgetry, but introduced it as one method of information retrieval.

Once again, we produced materials which are adaptable for other disciplines. Students were given a manual containing a structured search strategy with emphasis on the use of periodical indexes and their online data base sources in a number of health service-related fields.

Again we stressed active learning, reinforced by consultation with faculty. The librarian's role was that of a facilitator as students learned about the organization of the information retrieval system of a discipline.

Structuring of the computer search necessitates a more thorough consideration of the topic and more careful planning of search strategy than students usually employ when they undertake a manual search. The search results were often printed out only as abstract numbers, obliging students to return to the printed indexes for bibliographic information and the abstract summaries. Thus, they became familiar with the printed indexes, too. The computer search produced a nucleus of articles which gave students a starting place with which they could feel comfortable. Their initial efforts are more fruitful than in the usual random searching for information in printed indexes. A good deal of the frustration students experience in conducting searches in the printed indexes is eliminated.

The goals to be realized by our instruction in the Health Services Seminar were:
1. Making students familiar with a new method of searching for current research data.
2. Acquainting or reacquainting them with the use of the printed indexes and abstracts which are generated from computer data bases.
3. Developing in them an understanding of the organization of the literature of the sciences and social sciences of which the Health Services field is a part.

The library research portion of the class included a workshop in which students were introduced to the concept of data base searching. They examined pertinent printed indexes which they would use in connection with the computer search. Small group sessions were held to demonstrate online searching. This searching was pre-planned to show the development of a logical search.

Next, students were assigned to (1) search one of the topics discussed in the seminar in at least three of the printed indexes introduced in the manual and workshop (2) find one entry in each which pertained to the subject and (3) produce a bibliography containing three unabbreviated citations.

After each student had completed this assignment he met to discuss his proposed research topic with an instructor. Then student and librarian planned a search strategy on the chosen topic and went together to the terminal to run the data base search. After we had seen a few citations and determined that the search strategy was viable, we had the rest of the citations printed out as abstract numbers rather than full citations, obliging students to make use of the printed indexes for bibliographic information and abstracts. Students were aware of the high cost of searches and therefore seemed content to return to the printed indexes for further information.

By making the use of online data bases contingent upon a return to the printed index, we had introduced online searching as an instructional tool as well as a major research resource.

Just what did all this accomplish? We have noted the enthusiastic response of students, the willingness with which they have returned to use the printed indexes after completing a computer search and, in general, their improved skills at designing search strategy. Our conclusions are based on three evaluative measures: First, student perception of the workshop and data base search as described in the questionnaire which they answered; second, examination of each student's search strategy; third, analysis of the student's use of this strategy in the completed assignment.

Since computer searching provides us with a finite document with which we can measure the success of the research strategy, we can come to some very definite conclusions about the extent of student learning through this medium. We noted that students evidenced considerable ability in searching, analyzing, interpreting and relating data to a preconceived format. Their bibliographies were well selected and pertinent to their outlines.

From the first, our online search program has been tied to library instruction. Thus, we were able to move cautiously into a new service area and make it an integral part of our instructional and reference services gradually. The cost has not been great in dollars but the resultant prestige on campus and potential effectiveness of the new library service make it invaluable.

We have already revised the manual and restructured the learning experience for classes in psychology, social research, education and history. The inclusion of online searching convinced this nucleus of research-oriented faculty to incorporate library research instruction in their courses.

Partially as a result of this new gadget, the humanities faculty climbed aboard with enthusiasm for the next phase of our instructional development plan. They are working with us to include on-line searching in structured library components for their classes, as they set out this year to revamp their major curriculum into a sequential pattern.

The positive results of our program have been:
1. In classes using searching as an instructional tool, communication between faculty, students and librarians has become easier.
2. Students are involved in an active learning process as they conduct a structured search of a new information retrieval technology. They become proficient in the use of both hard copy and online periodical indexes.
3. Faculty interest is aroused by this new technology, and the library has achieved a more exciting image.

Just as in the case of the chemistry professors, other faculty members are impressed with what the new service has to offer. In a survey conducted in the fall of 1977 to which all faculty members responded, 38 out of 83 indicated an interest in the potential of this new service. Thirty-three of them were willing to participate in a workshop to learn more about the service. This climate has not diminished, instead, other faculty members have expressed a desire to become involved in the program. I hope this brief report has aroused your interest in the program, too, and you will consider implementing some form of it.

By now I have described to you a number of ways in which we at Lake Forest have responded to a cluster of recent academic innovations: faculty development, skills competence, course requirements, re-sequencing of major study program, and an advanced library technology. The atmosphere on our campus, and on many others, is one of eager acceptance of change. These changes have led to increasing faculty/student/librarian communication which aids in the development of library instruction materials and techniques. I have included the details of our instructional innovations in the hopes that if some of you in academic institutions large and small can make use of them in your programs, the progress we have made with our grant will be doubly justified, and you will have reaped some benefit from the taxpayers' money that we spent.

REFERENCES

Bayley, David H. "The Emptiness of Curriculum Reform." *Journal of Higher Education* 43 (November 1972):591-600.

Bok, Derek. "On the Purposes of Undergraduate Education." *Daedalus* 103 (Fall 1974):159-172.

Friedes, Thelma. *The Literature and Bibliography of the Social Sciences.* Los Angeles: Melville Publishing Co., 1973.

Knapp, Patricia. *The Monteith College Library Experiment.* New York: Scarecrow Press, 1966.

Knapp, Sara. "The Reference Interview in the Computer Based Setting," *RQ* 17 (Summer 1978):320-324.

McInnis, Raymond G. *New Perspectives for Reference Service in Academic Libraries.* Westport, CT: Greenwood Press, 1978.

Mead, Margaret. "Why is Education Obsolete?" *Harvard Business Review* 36 (1958):23-34+.

Schiefelbein, Susan. "Confusion at Harvard: What Makes an 'Educated Man?'" *Saturday Review* 5 (April 1, 1978):12-20.

Somerville, Arleen. "The Place of the Reference Interview in Computer Searching: The Academic Setting," *On Line* 1 (October 1977): 14-23.

THE CHANGING ROLES AND EXPECTATIONS OF ACADEMIC LIBRARIANS

A.P. Marshall
Reference Librarian, Center of Educational Resources
Eastern Michigan University

Over the past 40 years I have observed many changes in the roles played by librarians in the academic setting. Though change is constant in almost any setting, there has been an acceleration in this profession which deserves some attention. The rapid increases in printed materials, the application of computer technology to library management, the availability of better prepared and educated personnel, and the increased expectations of college and university administrators to utilize all the human resources at their disposal, have all contributed to drastic changes within libraries. Add to these the large increases in college and university enrollments which prompted additional concerns for services and cost reduction practices and some changes in expectations are even more understandable.

One has only to research the changes in librarian preparation over that period to realize that this is not a static profession. In the earlier years library schools admitted students with high school diplomas. Any work beyond that was a bonus. Many librarians who were responsible for servicing the needs of college and university students, even as late as the 1930s, had only received one or two years of college training themselves. As library schools began to demand a baccalaureate degree, the reward for the fifth year was another bachelors degree. It was not until the war years of the 1940s that the masters degree became acceptable and appropriate for the fifth year of study. True some librarians studied a sixth year to obtain the masters degree, and fewer still the doctorate, but many received their graduate degrees in other fields when they were so motivated. Others provided a rather satisfactory level of service with much less than the minimal expectations of today.

According to the thirty-first edition of the *American Library Directory*,[1] there are 1,708 college and university libraries operating in the United States (1978). Each strives to provide the best services possible within its means, and to reflect the academic environment of which it is a part. The size and purpose are determined by a variety of factors resulting from differences in physical arrangement, the way services are offered, and often, the growth patterns as determined by college administrations and faculties, and the general orientation of students who matriculate.

The constant changes do not affect the similarities which exist. These are usually determined by librarians and administrators who dream of building more viable collections and programs to serve the present and the future as they see it. The rippling effects of new equipment, introduced primarily during the last two or three decades, have altered professional requirements and responsibilities. These include: 1) increases in the entrance level training of the professional staff, 2) alterations of access systems which reflect availability of printed and non-printed materials, 3) meeting the demands of larger numbers of students, and 4) the rapid development of new professional skills requirements.

The higher levels of formal education brought to the campuses by librarians have increased their expectations as responsibilities changed. Library administrators, who are often as well learned as their colleagues in other offices, are being called upon to provide counsel and input on a variety of campus concerns, many with no direct relationships to their major responsibilities. Library staff members, whether they have official faculty recognition or not, often serve along with other faculty on various sanctioned committees concerned with student affairs, instructional problems, or wherever their interests, expertise, and/or abilities are considered useful. They are more likely to be members of faculty unions than to be organized into separate ones where unionization has taken place. Their professional assignments often broaden in response to their clamor for shared administrative responsibility in the governance of the institutions.

Even within libraries there has been a gradual change in the way librarians view their responsibilities. One of the major causes is the development and use of more sophisticated tools to make the rapidly expanding information available. As each subject area witnesses a growth of published information, additional tools become necessary so that quick and easy access is provided. Complete self-sufficiency in the use of library information resources, however, is next to impossible for the average student, and even faculty. Recognizing this, librarians have come to see library use instruction as a natural part of the educational process, and few college libraries are without some method of acquainting students with basic reference tools and an overview of research techniques. By so doing they are carving a place for themselves in the total educational process.

In order to get a pictute of similarities as well as differences in today's libraries, a questionnaire was developed and sent to 220 randomly selected college and university libraries during the summer of 1977, about 13 percent of the total. It was believed that such a sampling would provide some knowledge of trends among libraries as they adjust to institutional changes. Responses were received from 192 libraries, a return of 87 percent, and representing 11.3 percent of U.S. academic libraries. A decision was made to keep the questionnaire as simple as possible, structuring questions so that they could be answered in most instances by checking the right answer, while a few required the writing of one or two words or numbers.

Though there were only 10 major questions, the effective number of answers required was 38. Not all questions were answered by all the respondents. The sampling, does, however, represent a cross-section of baccalaureate institutions in all parts of the United States. Table 1 shows the distribution of respondents.

Table 1. Distribution of Libraries

Geographical Location	Number Responding	Percentage Responses
Southern	65	33.9
Eastern	42	21.9
Western	34	17.7
Midwestern	49	25.5
No Indication	2	1.0
	192	100.0

Librarians answer to a variety of senior officers, dependent upon the organizational structure of the college or university. The largest group, however, reports to the Academic Vice President, or in some instances, the Vice Chancellor. Four libraries indicated that they report to a non-academic officer, while three report to "other officers of the institution." Table 2 shows the number and percentages in each category.

Table 2. Supervisory Officers

Officer	Number	Percent
President (or Chancellor)	17	8.9
Academic Vice President (or Vice Chancellor)	115	59.8
Dean of Faculties	15	7.8
Provost or Similar Officer	17	8.9
Academic Dean	21	10.0
Non-Academic Officer	4	2.1
Other	3	1.6
	192	100.0

The three libraries which checked "Other," provided the titles of 1) Dean of Learning Resources and Telecommunications, 2) Vice President for Educational Services (Library, Telecommunications, ROTC, Archives, AV Services), and 3) Executive Dean. One respondent indicated reporting to the Assistant Academic Vice President, commenting that the "Academic Vice President thinks his span of control is too broad to include the Director of Libraries." A library director in the Eastern Region reported that he answers to the Assistant Provost for academic support. Another director reported that he is responsible to the Provost "for matters of professional personnel," and to the Academic Dean for "matters of policy and budget." Another librarian reports to the Provost, but "on some matters I deal directly with the President."

Respondents represented 102 publicly supported (53.1 percent) and 75 privately supported (39.1 percent) institutions. Fifteen failed to indicate the kind of control. Questionnaires were sent to baccalaureate degree-granting institutions only, 25 percent of which offered only the initial four-year degree, and 36 percent at least one doctorate. Table 3 provides a summary of institutional types by degrees offered.

Table 3. Level of Degree Offerings

Level	Number	Percent
4-Year Baccalaureate Only	48	25.0
Baccalaureate through Masters	61	31.8
Baccalaureate through Doctoral	70	36.4
No Indication	13	6.8
	192	100.0

Staff sizes varied greatly, with the largest number having from one to nine members, and the second largest having from ten to nineteen members, all of which are exclusive of the director. Table 4 provides a breakdown of staff size among responding libraries.

Table 4. Professional Staff Sizes

Categories	Number of Librarians	Percent
1 – 9	93	48.4
10 – 19	36	18.8
20 – 39	26	13.5
40 – 69	25	13.0
70 – 89	2	1.0
Over 90	7	3.7
No Indication	3	1.6
	192	100.0

Two questions were designed to determine whether library directors and professional staff members have opportunities for input when general institutional policies are being considered. A majority have such opportunities, but the survey indicated that 28 percent of administrators and 24 percent of professional staff members are not consulted on general institutional policies. Table 5 provides a breakdown of answers to those questions.

Table 5. Opportunities for Institutional Input

	Directors	Percent	Staff	Percent
Yes	145	75.5	138	71.9
No	46	24.0	54	28.1
No Indication	1	.5	0	0.0
	192	100.0	192	100.0

Participation in professional organizations is considered by many to be one of the best means of continuing education for librarians. Some institutions encourage participation in special interest groups outside of the library field. The question was asked as follows: "Are the library director and members of the library staff encouraged to participate in professional organizations, local, state, and national, which have libraries as their major interest?" followed by a second one, "Are professional staff members encouraged to participate in professional activities and organizations other than those primarily concerned with library services?" No effort was made to determine the kinds of encouragement provided. As might be expected, a larger number of institutions encourage participation in library-related activities and organizations than they do in non-related. Table 6 is a tabular breakdown of answers to these questions.

Table 6. Professional Activity Encouragement

	Library Related		Non-Library Related	
	Number	Percent	Number	Percent
Yes	180	93.8	146	76.0
No	11	5.7	39	20.3
No answer	1	.5	7	3.7
	192	100.0	192	100.0

One question sought to determine the extent of unionization among librarians. The question was asked, "Is the library professional staff organized into a union?" Twenty-four (12.5 percent) of the respondents indicated that they are unionized, while 166 (71.0 percent) answered negatively. Of the 24, only four (16.5 percent) were in exclusive library unions. The other 20 (80.8 percent) were represented in faculty unions.

Rutherford Rogers and David C. Weber offered an opinion in *University Library Administration* (1971) regarding faculty rank: "The arguments for faculty rank rest on such factors as full participation in the educational enterprise and recognition of librarianship as a learned discipline."[2] According to the survey, library directors usually have some form of recognition as faculty, often through a teaching department. In some institutions all administrators, including those in the library, are denied academic rank. Table 7 shows how this question was answered.

Table 7. Academic Rank for Administrators

	Rank	Percent	By Dept.	Percent	Excluded	Percent
Yes	141	73.4	57	29.7	44	22.9
No	49	25.6	72	37.5	28	14.6
No Indication	2	1.0	63	32.8	120	62.5
	192	100.0	192	100.0	192	100.0

Another question sought to determine the number of professional library staff members with faculty rank. A majority, 139 (72.4 percent) indicated that some librarians do hold rank, while 47 (24.5 percent) answered negatively. All professional librarians hold rank in 78 institutional libraries (40.6 percent).

Asked to indicate how promotions are granted, 90 institutions (46.9 percent) marked "Same as faculty," while "Special consideration geared to librarians" was marked by 21 institutions (10.0 percent). "No set policy" was indicated by 24 (12.5 percent), and 10 (5.2 percent) indicated that other methods are used.[3]

Another part of the question asked, "If librarians do have faculty rank, what does it mean?" The majority, 112 (58.3 percent), indicated that librarians have "full calendar year appointments," while 32 (16.7 percent) indicated that the two-semester base was used. Salary scales match those of faculty in 50 libraries, compared to 55 (28.6 percent) with differing scales. Further, 42 institutions reported that salary scales are "established differently from faculty" with only 12 (6.3 percent) checking "computed from basic teacher salaries."

In an effort to determine the expectations of library staff members concerning instruction in library use, the question was asked, "Does library and/or institutional policy encourage promotion of activities to increase student use and understanding of library services?" Though the question was rather general by design, 174 (90.6 percent) respondents answered affirmatively with only seven (3.6 percent) answering negatively. Related questions concerning the nature of offerings showed that 60 (35.0 percent of those offering courses) offer credit courses, 50 (28.7 percent) of which are elective and only four (2.3 percent) have required courses. Noncredit elective courses are offered by 13 (7.5 percent) institutions, with six (3.4 percent) making them a requirement. Short courses "of one to four weeks duration" are offered as electives by 17 (9.8 percent) institutions, while four (2.3 percent) make them a requirement.

A majority of libraries (167 or 87.0 percent) respond to teachers' requests to talk to classes, while cooperative planning of course work with teachers is practiced by 128 libraries (66.7 percent). Institutional orientation programs involve librarians in 143 (74.5 percent). Other kinds of involvement were reported by 33 (17.7 percent) respondents.

Conclusions

Assuming the sampling process to have some validity, college and university librarians are being given greater opportunities to exercise their abilities and interests in higher education. This is being achieved to a great extent without unionization, but there is no doubt that the spectre of the union movement is reflected on some campuses where opportunities for greater participation are offered.

Earlier in the century when library collections reflected minimal support on many campuses, librarians believed that their best chance to influence greater financial support was to report directly to the President. A general increase in resources over the past three decades and the concomitant growth in administrative structure and expectations have meant a shift in assigned responsibilities. Now it is generally acceptable for library directors to report to Vice Presidents, Vice Chancellors, Academic Deans, or Provosts, but always rather close to the power structure. That so many institutions have an array of such titles is, in itself, a testimony to the changing times.

Another indication of the important roles of librarians on campuses in the United States is the increasing number who hold academic rank. Though granting the same status, terms of employment, and promotion opportunities as the teaching faculties is still not a universal practice, substantial progress is evident. It is believed important that 46.9 percent of respondents indicated that promotions are granted to librarians in the same way that they are granted to teaching faculty. Though 58.3 percent reported 12-month appointments, the 16.7 percent enjoying two-semester appointments may show a significant trend. Unfortunately, the questionnaire did not distinguish those institutions which do not offer summer work.

The proliferation of resources, together with the tools to use them, is seen as making the teaching of library usage mandatory. The trend toward credit and non-credit courses, along with short courses, affects 51.7 percent of responding libraries. This may also reflect a strong desire by librarians to contribute more meaningfully to the teaching/learning process.

This study, though not definitive, provides some indication of trends toward a stronger, more viable profession. Perhaps the greatest conclusion to be reached from it is that so many changes are taking place that members of the profession must be committed to continuing education while developing new applications of their knowledge. It may also mean that a higher degree of learning creates a desire for more challenges, whether within or without the library profession. Certainly the idea of over-preparedness is disappearing as new challenges are seen as beneficial to the development of both library and institutional services.

FOOTNOTES

1. *American Library Directory*. 31st edition. Edited by Jaques Cattell Press. (New York: R.R. Bowker Company, 1978.) p. xi.

2. Rogers, Rutherford D. and Weber, David C. *University Library Administration*. (New York: The H.W. Wilson Company, 1971.) 53 pp.

3. This section of the test was answered by 145 respondents, compared with 139 who reported having faculty rank for librarians.

THE FOUR R's:
IMPLICATIONS FOR LIBRARY SERVICES

Cleo Treadway
Director
Tusculum College Library

Josephine Bradley
Assistant Professor, Sociology/Social Services
Tusculum College

Introduction

Two years ago, on the last day of the seventh Annual LOEX conference, I was sitting where you are now becoming more and more frustrated as I heard reference after reference to "they" – meaning our classroom faculty – and "their" lack of understanding of and commitment to the use of library resources by their students. Although I myself have been guilty of very similar remarks about our classroom instructors, at that time I grew more and more defensive for "them"; I was disturbed that "they" were not there to defend themselves.

I can remember voicing these concerns to Beverly Lynch on that day, two years ago, and suggesting that we should have a conference which included them – our classroom and administrative colleagues.

Last year an English professor from Tusculum College attended the Eighth Annual LOEX conference with me. A year ago last fall I took our academic Dean and a sociology professor with me to the Bibliographic Instruction Workshop at Earlham College. Last month a history professor and a new librarian on our staff attended the 1979 Earlham Workshop. These three faculty development activities have proved to be extremely beneficial for Tusculum College – both in progress toward the realization of institutional goals and for the goals of the library.

This year I have another Tusculum College professor with me, and I am very proud and pleased that she has agreed to share the speaker's platform. Jo Bradley and I are going to be talking about reform and renewal in higher education and its implications for library services. We will also be outlining what we think is an ideal program of library services; and then we will describe the situation as it really is at Tusculum College.

The Four R's: Implications for Library Services

Higher education has a long and continuing history of reform and renewal. Indeed, all institutions experience change. Some of the changes are innovative and constructive; some are faddish and counter-productive. Some reforms are dictated by the changing times; some are instituted simply for the sake of change. Within the academic community, reactions to new programs and new directions vary considerably, ranging from apathy to over-reaction, from debate and controversy to understanding and acceptance.

What have been the results of the many attempts at reform and renewal? Certainly the problems have not been eliminated -- perhaps they have been compounded.

In a recent study, *Strategic Policy Changes at Private Colleges*, Richard Anderson from Columbia University reported that many of the small private colleges that reacted to the 1960s by liberalizing their policies and relaxing their standards are now experiencing a deterioration in student scholarship and morale, in the quality of teaching, and in campus community spirit. In changing their mission, these colleges lost their unique characteristics and are now having difficulty recruiting and keeping students.[1] And recruiting students is, indeed, one of the problems for which the academic community continues to seek solutions -- positive results.

I suspect all of you would agree that the desired results will not be realized until all constituents of the community plan and work together – not reacting to change, but effecting well-planned change to meet the changing times.

Let me illustrate with a parable.

The Parable of the Four R's

Once upon a time there was a bunch of people stuck in a hole. Attempts were made by various individuals to get out of the hole (reform and renewal), such as desperate arm flapping, jumping, meditation and levitation (reactions). This went on for hundreds of years, until they had tried everything except helping each other out, so they helped each other out of the hole (results).

What are the implications of this parable for library services?

I considered labeling this presentation "Reform and Renewal – So What!" Because in my opinion, academic library services have not been significantly affected by the various attempts at reform and renewal. Certainly we have experienced change, and we continue to make changes in our libraries – changes that reflect the changing times – but this is just good librarianship. For example, our training has prepared us to develop collections to meet the changing needs of a diversified student population and to meet the demands of an expanded curriculum. Our training has prepared us to take advantage of new technology in both the bibliographic services as well as in the business operations of our libraries. But these and similar changes have not altered the mission of academic libraries nor the basic elements of good librarianship.

On the other hand, I am convinced that creative and dynamic library services can and should play a large part in effecting significant improvements in higher education. Penny Abell, in her remarks at the 1978 ACRL Boston conference, said that librarians "need to exercise the initiative required not only to respond to change, but also to effect change."[2] I concur.

If the mission of your library is to enhance the teaching/learning process, then your library is – or should be – planning with other academic units on your campus toward the common goal of better educated students. If your philosophy is one of educational librarianship, then you and your librarian colleagues will accept the responsibility of participating with classroom faculty and administrators in academic planning and in the shaping of the curriculum; you will be there during committee meetings and task force sessions to temper the sometimes narrow, tunnel-vision of the classroom specialist with the viewpoint of a generalist and from an interdisciplinary perspective.

Let's look again at "The Parable of the Four R's" and consider its implications for Library Services.

The Parable of the Four R's: Implications for Library Services

Once upon a time -- and continuing into the now – there was a bunch of people stuck in a hole; that is to say -- higher education was beset with many problems.

Once upon a time -- and continuing into the now – attempts were made by various individuals to get out of the hole; that is to say – many attempts were made by administrators and classroom faculty and library faculty at reform and renewal.

Once upon a time -- and continuing into the now – the reactions to the attempts at reform and renewal took a variety of forms.

And this went on for hundreds of years – and will continue until our arm flapping and meditation become cooperative efforts; until we work together, rather than in isolation, and help each other out. And thus shall we effect enhancement of education through optimum utilization of resources.

This parable of the four R's describes the underlying philosophy of a program which is developing on the Tusculum College campus. Tusculum College is a small, private, church-related college with a faculty of 30 and a student enrollment of 450 -- an enrollment which is slowly climbing back to a peak enrollment of 600. Tusculum has not escaped the hasty attempts at reform and renewal nor the consequences of these changes, such as open admissions, relaxed core requirements, dilution of the liberal arts, and diminishing use of library resources due to the increasing dependence upon textbooks for resource material.

In our lengthy campus discussions of the problems that confront us, we frequently lose sight of the fact that we are not struggling with something new, but that "the terms of the present debate have been central to every critical examination of the academy for at least 80 years."[3]

The Division of Library Services at Tusculum is one of seven academic divisions. Each of the academic divisions, as well as selected students, participated in designing a program which has been funded by the National Endowment for the Humanities and the Council on Library Resources and which is expected to effect optimum utilization of library resources in the teaching/learning process. Our program was not manufactured to match a funding agency's guidelines. On the contrary, our needs and our resources matched an available opportunity -- an opportunity that would enable us to move more rapidly in a direction we had previously chosen. Needless to say, we are grateful to the Council and to the Endowment for this opportunity.

Being the recipient of an award of this nature is a humbling -- an awesome experience. Now that we have been given the resources to effect change, can we do it? On a recent library questionnaire one of our classroom faculty suggested that we need less talk and more action! Again I ask the question: can we do it? Do you find, as I do, that the "talking" is easier than the "doing?"

Tusculum's program involves three approaches to the enhancement of education:
1. Creation of an environment which is intellectually stimulating; an environment which will foster inquiry and will invite self-initiated exploration of resources.
2. Establishment of active library/classroom liaisons in all major disciplines.
3. Development and implementation of a comprehensive program of sequential, course-related, curriculum-integrated bibliographic instruction.

Although the three approaches overlap and have features in common, each serves a distinct function in the accomplishment of the primary goal -- enhancement of education through optimum utilization of library resources.

This, then, is our plan at Tusculum College. There is nothing new in it. It simply represents what academic libraries are all about. It is an ideal toward which we are progressing.

Just a word about bibliographic instruction. Those of you who know me know that I am firmly committed to bibliographic instruction and that I advocate sequential, course-related, curriculum-integrated bibliographic instruction. I'm not sure that I agree with one of our colleagues who said that bibliographic instruction is one of the liberal arts.[4] But I do strongly believe that bibliographic instruction is an essential ingredient of a liberating education and will play a large part in ensuring optimum utilization of library resources. On the other hand, bibliographic instruction will not be effective in isolation. Remember that it is only one of three approaches in our program.

The Carnegie Foundation for the Advancement of Teaching has said that "the curriculum is . . . not the most important aspect of undergraduate education. The most important is the quality of the faculty . . . . "[5] If classroom faculty were all of the quality and caliber of Jo Bradley, Tusculum College would have no major problems. I am both proud and pleased that Jo has agreed to be here today. She is going to "tell it like it is" at Tusculum.

Total commitment to and involvement in curriculum planning with a librarian was indeed a new experience for me! Prior to involvement in bibliographic instruction with Tusculum College librarians, I had been accustomed to making assignments which required minimal use of the library by students. Very little consideration had been given to more unique, and well planned approaches to library use. While I had a commitment to use the library as a supportive facility, but not as an integral part of my courses, I had given little consideration to any further use of the library. I knew, however, that I could not support the positions of the students who had interviewed me during the search process at Tusculum College: 1) instructors generally do not give library assignments to students; 2) the library is too inadequate to seriously consider using it for course assignments. Both of these positions went against my own personal experience and philosophy about libraries and perhaps contributed, therefore, to my involvement in the Library Service Enhancement Program during the 1977--78 school year and presently.

In initial preparation for the first quarter at Tusculum College, the library became an immediate resource. In a preliminary tour of the library I did indeed make several interesting observations and discoveries: 1) it was much smaller than most of the libraries I was personally used to; 2) there was a very limited social services collection and subscription to only one professional journal, *Social*

Casework; 3) there was an adequate collection in Sociology and Psychology; 4) reference tools were better than anticipated. The greatest surprise was a discovery of the *Encyclopedia of Social Work* dating back to 1937. Having made the discovery that, while small in scope, there were indeed adequate resources that could be utilized, I proceeded to follow my usual trend and make the usual reading assignments and the usual term papers.

It was at this point that I was introduced to the concept of bibliographic instruction and joint course planning with the librarian. Of course, my immediate response was "You have got to be kidding. What can a librarian tell me except where the books are located and how to order more books and journals?" However, after the introduction to the notion of bibliographic instruction and joint course planning, my attitude and enthusiasm changed. Suddenly, I recognized the fact that my course assignments could become more interesting, individualized, challenging and more importantly, more worthwhile in helping students learn to appreciate the role of the library in their future professional development. The hidden agenda was that each time the student used the library, he/she would come away with a new experience and appreciation of what a small college library has to offer. Therefore, in approaching this daring undertaking, the Director of the Library Service Enhancement Program and I spent many hours together developing tasks to help students in learning and improving research skills, becoming familiar with sources, learning how to distinguish high quality from low quality materials and learning how to synthesize from diverse sources.

That most students enrolled in "Society, Culture and Personality," "Community Organization" and "Introduction to Social Services" would be negative and ill-informed, possess less than desired skills in library utilization was recognized by those involved in planning. Further, we were aware that students would resist increased use of the library. It was common knowledge that few students knew what reference sources were available to them, how to use the Interlibrary Loan Program, possessed limited techniques of search strategy or used the library except for dire emergencies.

The purposes of sequential bibliographic instruction for sociology and social service majors, therefore, are twofold: "to ensure the bibliographic competency of all graduating sociology and social services majors; to enable students to more efficiently and effectively locate and use information sources, thus enhancing their college education and better preparing them for the independent research required both for successful graduate work and for remaining abreast of current developments as working professionals."[6]

Instructional objectives were set up in three (3) phases: Phase I is designed for freshmen students and has as its purpose: "to acquaint beginning college freshmen with library facilities, organization patterns, circulation procedures, and staff; and to enable them to locate and to use general information sources."[7] Phase II is designed "to build directly on the bibliographic competencies developed through Phase I instruction and will be implemented as an integral part of a three course humanities sequence which all sophomores (150–180) are required to take."[8] Phase III "is designed to develop the ability of junior and senior students to conduct scholarly research at an advanced and professional level within each one's particular area of concentration."[9] [See Appendix.]

Prior to the Fall Quarter of 1977–78 school year, the Director of LSEP and I began to meet to review the courses individually and collectively. This included the proposed course syllabi, textbooks and assignments. The textbook, *Tactics and Techniques of Community Organization* by Cox et al, which was used for the Community Organization course, actually devoted an entire chapter to the library as a resource for persons working as community organizers, planners, etc.[10] The Sociology text, *Sociology* by Ian Robertson, also included in the Appendix a section on "Techniques of Library Research."[11]

Building upon these class oriented references on library use, assignments were developed and included such things as photo-essays (which required not only a picture about a sociological concept, but also references supporting or explaining that concept), short reports, annotated bibliographies, grants, term papers, reports demonstrating research strategies. Students had, and will continue to have, questions on their examinations pertaining to information from bibliographic instruction sessions, handouts, etc.

The teaching strategies used by the librarian to help prepare students with the necessary tools to complete the assignments included: "classroom lectures and demonstration of search techniques illustrated with transparencies and supplemented by printed handouts; small group seminars in the library; library "lab" sessions with brief lectures or demonstration followed by supervised library search required to complete a class assignment; self instructional units; class handouts which consisted of bibliographies or other printed guides prepared by the library and distributed in class by the instructor; detailed reference counseling which consisted of reference appointments with individual students; flow charts to demonstrate possible search strategies; field trips to a nearby University library for demonstration of data bases and reference materials not available at Tusculum College."[12]

The degree of planning that occurred during the first year has not taken place this year (1978–79). Timing has perhaps been the greatest enemy, i.e., for meetings with the library staff and myself to plan for courses. Also, more time and effort have been devoted to developing a similar involvement with the new General Studies course. Many of the senior students had gone through bibliographic instruction in the initial phase and can now perform on their own with more individual work with the Reference librarians and handouts prepared by the library. Assignments given to juniors, as well as seniors, have focused on developing their abilities to "conduct scholarly research at an advanced and professional level within each one's particular area of concentration."[13]

From their assignments, such as presentations on various counseling models, we have been able to identify areas in which resource materials are needed. For example, a very useful practice model in social work and psychology is the problem-solving model. Besides Perlman's book, *Social Casework: A Problem-Solving Model*, no other major resource is available.[14] Since this is a pertinent area, we can now look for additional inclusions.

Senior social work students enrolled in the Social Services Practicum must complete a major research project in their selected area of practice. They are being encouraged to do some original research which includes a review of the literature and the use of the scientific method. They have been encouraged to do bibliography cards, sorting them out according to what is available at Tusculum's library and what is not available, then scheduling an individual appointment with the Director of the Library or the reference librarian to see what can be ordered through Interlibrary loan. If necessary, excursions to the University of Tennessee or East Tennessee State libraries have been arranged so that students might use reference works not available at Tusculum.

Students enrolled in the "Contemporary Social Issues" course must write a Position Paper on a contemporary social problem using the latest information available on the topic and work back to the primary source. Another assignment requiring library utilization is the weekly analysis. Each assignment requires the use of at least two library sources. Students are, on selected assignments, given credit for inclusion of these sources as well as credit for the proper citation of the sources.

Students have had the opportunity to evaluate the process of bibliographic instruction throughout the two years. I have found in evaluating the process that students who are social work majors are now accustomed to having to use the library. There has been noticeable improvement in the caliber of papers turned in. However, there are some who still resist having to use the library "so much."

Students in Social Work are now unable to say, "but there are no resources available." The available resources have increased tremendously this year thanks to a grant from the Student Government Association and private grants.

Students in the Social Services Practicum have utilized the library for ordering films, research on counseling techniques (such as values clarification, art therapy, group processes and activities and audio visual presentations). This course, perhaps more so than the others, is beginning to demonstrate to the students a new awareness of available library materials, how to use a library effectively in the delivery of services to their clients, of the importance of integrating material from class to class and from library assignment to class assignments. The nature of some of the placements, such as the school system and mental retardation facilities, demand planning of activities by the students which in turn require utilization of the library.

I have found that by designating all assignments at the beginning of the quarter on a separate assignment sheet, giving dates due, the number of sources to be utilized, means that students can plan more effectively for the course and hopefully, more appropriately for effective use of the library.

I feel that bibliographic instruction is more effective when planned ahead jointly by the librarian and instructors. This includes whether the librarian is going to come to the class, or handouts will be used or individualized conferences will be needed. This, I feel, makes for better use of the librarian and helps the instructor in planning and the student in meeting the course assignments in the desired manner.

Use of the library and its staff in this manner has also provided us with areas of identified resource needs. In social services there is a definite need for materials on research that has been done and is being done within the field and group work.

For the future, one can only see continued use of the library and the librarians in course planning and bibliographic instruction. A mini-thesis for students enrolled in the Social Services Practicum will be a requirement next year. This will accomplish the objective mentioned earlier: that students should be able to conduct scholarly research at an advanced and professional level. The objectives of the mini-thesis are threefold: 1) to help students prepare for social work practice; 2) to help them understand the importance of making worthwhile contributions to continuing social work education; and 3) to prepare them for graduate study. With the students' permission, the papers will be used as resource materials for other social service classes including Methods of Research.

What I have done up to this point is to share with you the experiences of one faculty member who has gotten involved in bibliographic instruction and joint-curriculum planning. Let me briefly share with you reasons I feel that other faculty members perhaps do not participate in such joint endeavors. In order to do this, I must first of all pose a twofold question for your consideration -- this is: "Is the goal of the librarians to have the faculty actively participate in bibliographic instruction and joint-curriculum planning or to alienate the faculty?" Let's assume that you would answer the first part of the question with a resounding "yes" and the second part with a resounding "no." However, as a faculty member, if I were not already committed to library support, after listening to what has been stated in the presentations at this conference, I would not be willing to participate. It seems to me that more emphasis has been placed on the latter part of the question. To borrow a phrase from Rose's book *We and They*, I and other faculty members feel like a *they*.[15] For example, it has been continuously stated that "they (meaning faculty) must change *their* attitudes." And I have heard you expound upon "what *we* (meaning librarians) want to do," and "how little *they* know about the library." The attitude I felt coming across was "we (again meaning librarians) must teach *them* something." After listening to this I began to experience certain emotions -- defensiveness, hostility, and anger. It seemed that people were saying that faculty members were "incompetent" to perform their jobs effectively, and perhaps that is the crux of the problem. That is, maybe it is not just the attitude of faculty members that must be changed, but also the attitude of librarians. It appears that the two factions on the college campus who are in need of one another are too busy blaming each other for failures and problems. If one looks at the problem from the sociological and psychological perspectives, two factors are involved – fear and change. The faculty fear that the librarians are passing judgment and saying let us show you how to teach your classes/make assignments/be more competent. While librarians fear rejection of their credibility and acceptance of them as equals by faculty members. Both fear *change*. For change means giving up what is comfortable to do, what is "unknown," and to be innovative.

On large college/university campuses faculty members are confronted with the syndrome of "publish or perish." The question is no longer "are you effective as a teacher?" but, "how many papers have you published?" On small college campuses you are expected to be all things to all people with little time for planning outside of what one has to do for classes, committee meetings, advising students, etc. Time, or lack of time, is a major factor. Joint-planning is time consuming – it cannot be done in one day or one session.

Another thought occurs to me. Although librarians talk a lot about bibliographic instruction, no one bothers to explain to the faculty what bibliographic instruction means. And librarians continue to complain that "they refuse to get involved" -- or "they don't know...."

Perhaps some old-fashioned problem-solving techniques will help us solve our mutual problems.

Briefly:
a) Define the problem -- what is the problem; what is needed -- Is it how to involve the faculty in bibliographic instruction, or is it how to involve the faculty and librarians jointly in bibliographic instruction?
b) Make a needs assessment to find out what the faculty needs -- don't tell them -- let them tell you.
c) Develop goals and alternatives based upon results of the needs assessment.
d) Implement goals and alternatives.
e) Feedback and evaluation.

While this may not be a panacea, it may be a start. The beauty of the dream of optimum utilization of resources is that it can, with well thought-out approaches and with openness among faculty and librarians, become a reality.

Conclusion

Yesterday is our experience; tomorrow is our hope; and today is our trying to get from one to the other. It is helpful to us during this period of "trying to get from one to the other" to review the experiences of the past -- to review the successes and failures of our program to date. Our report to the Council on Library Resources at the end of the LSEP grant year included observations about both the strengths and the weaknesses of our program. You may find portions of this report of interest to you as you return to programs on your own campuses.

The Council asked us to comment in our final report about the nature and extent of faculty participation and cooperation. This was our response.[16]

> Classroom faculty and administrators have readily agreed with the rationale for and general goals of the program. Obtaining passive support is not difficult when only verbal assent is required. However, active support is not as readily forthcoming. Participation from the faculty was at varying levels of intensity. In some cases the classroom faculty enthusiastically and with initiative entered into planning with the library faculty. In other cases the classroom faculty politely cooperated -- at time requiring some gentle

prodding. In all cases, the year provided valuable learning experiences and resulted in a heightened awareness of the needs of students and of ways to meet those needs.

Obtaining active and aggressive faculty support is not so much difficult as it is slow and tenuous. A variety of circumstances account for less than enthusiastic faculty attitudes.

1. Inadequate ground work (consciousness-raising) by the library staff.
2. Lack of understanding of the need for, the purpose of, the opportunities for, the advantages of, and the methods of bibliographic instruction.
3. Lack of a successful model to demonstrate the value of bibliographic instruction.
4. Preoccupation of both thought and time with committee meetings and with campus politics.
5. A narrow approach to education.
6. Reluctance to devote already crowded class time to bibliographic instruction.
7. In a few cases, lack of concern about improving the teaching/learning process.

In our final report we were asked to list the special staff skills required to carry out a program which would more closely integrate library services with the total educational program. We responded, with the full realization that our staff is lacking in the breadth and depth of desirable skills.

Special staff skills

1. A broad knowledge of the field of higher education – goals, trends, governance, seats of power, idiosyncracies, current developments
2. Knowledge of institutional philosophy of education, goals and policies, current curriculum discussions
3. Collegiality with classroom faculty and administrators
4. Scholarship
5. Library research skills in all disciplines
6. Knowledge and application of sound educational principles and techniques
7. Successful classroom teaching experience
8. Knowledge of needs of students and faculty for library services

9. Creativeness; imagination; openness to new ideas
10. Middle management techniques; ability to present and to defend a well-developed plan at the right time to the right persons
11. Patience to proceed slowly and methodically
12. Perseverance to accept set-backs, to begin again, to evaluate and re-evaluate, to revise
13. Follow-through

We were also asked what priority our faculty would assign the new activities developed under the LSEP grant. This was, and is, a difficult question to answer. A realistic answer is that activities promoting optimum utilization of library resources have not taken top priority with our classroom faculty and administrators. And our new Instructional/Public Services Librarian has already expressed frustration because, as she expressed it, during "my first two months . . . I had neither time nor opportunity to do any extensive preparations for bibliographic instruction for the spring quarter." On the other hand, faculty development activities made possible by the Endowment and the Council have already produced some exciting results and have engendered the hope that priorities will change. Following participation in the Earlham College workshop last month, Dr. Donal Sexton, Professor of History, and Dr. Vivienne Dickson, Instructional/Public Services Librarian, sent to the Tusculum faculty a memorandum entitled "Thoughts on Bibliographic Instruction at Tusculum College." The following statements were included in their faculty memo.

> We came away from the conference convinced that Tusculum faculty should do more in the way of bibliographic instruction than it presently does . . . .
>
> Tusculum's library has the staff, facilities and materials to sustain such a program as Earlham's, but the faculty and student body generally have not made full use of them . . . .
>
> With thought and preparation, Tusculum could build a bibliographic instruction program as successful as Earlham's and suitable to its own needs.

This is exciting. This is progress. This supports my belief that, as our program becomes broader in scope and more firmly established, it will be a high priority for administrators, faculty, and students. This is not to say that I expect a program to be "written in stone." I suspect that no program should be considered established until it has been included in written curriculum policies and requirements; and even then, that a turnover in administrators and/or faculty will mean beginning anew to establish portions of the program. Moreover, even an established program will require continuous nudging, prodding, planning, guiding, and evaluating.

We believe that optimum utilization of library resources will enhance the quality of teaching at Tusculum College and will heighten the learning experiences of Tusculum students. We believe that the program, as it becomes fully and firmly entrenched in the curriculum, will give Tusculum College -- and can give your college -- a distinguishing feature that colleges need today to attract and to keep students. We believe that enhancement of education through optimum utilization of library resources will be our uniqueness.

REFERENCES

1. Richard A. Anderson, *Strategic Policy Changes at Private Colleges* (New York: Teachers College Press, 1977) as discussed in "Colleges Found Paying Price for Improved Finances," *The Chronicle of Higher Education*, February 6, 1978, p. 13.

2. Millicent D. Abell, "The Changing Role of the Academic Librarian: Drift and Mastery," *College & Research Libraries*, March, 1979, p. 158.

3. Barry O'Connell, "Where Does Harvard Lead Us?" *Change*, September, 1978, p. 38.

4. Stanley E. Gwynn, "The Liberal Arts Function of the University Library," in Herman H. Fussler, ed., *The Function of the Library in the Modern College* (Chicago: University of Chicago Press, 1954), p. 42.

5. Carnegie Foundation for the Advancement of Teaching, *Missions of the College Curriculum* (San Francisco: Jossey-Bass, 1977), p. 7.

6. Tusculum College, "Library Service Enhancement Program Final Report: July 1, 1977 -- June 30, 1978," p. 13.

7. Tusculum College, "Proposal to the Council on Library Resources and the National Endowment for the Humanities," p. 8.

8. Ibid., p. 10.

9. Ibid., p. 11.

10. Fred M. Cox, et al, *Tactics and Techniques of Community Practice* (Itasca, Illinois: Peacock Publishers, 1977).

11. Ian Robertson, *Sociology* (New York: Worth, 1977).

12. Tusculum College, "Proposal . . . ," p. 12.

13. Tusculum College, "Library Services . . . ," p. 14.

14. Helen Harris Perlman, *Social Casework, a Problem-solving Process* (Chicago: University of Chicago Press, 1957).

15. Peter I. Rose, *They and We: Racial and Ethnic Relations in the United States* (New York: Random House, 1964).

16. The following statements have been excerpted and adapted from Tusculum College, "Library Service Enhancement Program Final Report: July 1, 1977 -- June 30, 1978," available on loan from LOEX.

APPENDIX I

Excerpted from **Sesquential Bibliographic Instruction for Sociology/Social Services Majors Tusculum College — Revised 6-5-78**

INSTRUCTIONAL OBJECTIVES

Phase I and Phase II omitted.

Phase III. Phase III is designed to develop the ability of junior and senior students to conduct scholarly research at an advanced and professional level within each one's particular area of concentration. Upon completion of Phase III instruction, students will understand the organization of the literature in their respective fields of study and will be familiar with its basic and more advanced bibliographic apparatus.

A. The student will demonstrate an understanding of the salient features of the following:

> *Encyclopedia of the Social Sciences*
> *International Encyclopedia of the Social Sciences*
> *Encyclopedia of Sociology*
> *Encyclopedia of Social Work*
> various dictionaries of sociology
> *Social Sciences Index*
> *PAIS*
> *Sociological Abstracts*

B. The student will demonstrate ability to adapt terminology used in a subject search of the literature to the varied terminology of different reference sources; e.g., card catalog, *Sociological Abstracts, Annual Review of Sociology, New York Times Index, Monthly Catalog,* etc.

C. The student will be able to locate and interpret statistics relevant to a problem.

D. The student will be able to locate published reviews of books in sociology and social services.

E. The student will be able to locate information about prominent sociologists, both past and present.

F. The student will demonstrate knowledge of the specialized bibliographic tools of sociology and social services which are available in the Tusculum library, e.g.

> *Handbook of Modern Sociology*
> *Handbook of Small Group Research*
> *Handbook of Social Psychology*
> *Handbook of Socialization Theory and Research*
> *Review of Child Development Research*
> *Catalog of Federal Domestic Assistance*
> *Foundation Directory*
> *Dictionary of Occupational Titles*
> *Occupational Outlook Handbook*

G. The student will demonstrate knowledge of important bibliographic tools not available in the Tusculum College library; e.g., *Social Sciences Citation Index, Dissertation Abstracts,* complete U.S. census files, other data bases.

H. The student will demonstrate an understanding of the importance of government publications to a study of current social problems and will be able to use *Monthly Catalog* to identify government documents relevant to a problem.

I. The student will demonstrate knowledge of the scope and special features of the major journals of sociology and social services.

J. The student will demonstrate an understanding of the cross disciplinary "relatedness" of research and will be able to use the bibliographic apparatus of other disciplines when appropriate; e.g., *Psychological Abstracts, Annual Review of Psychology, Current Index to Journals in Education, Congressional Quarterly.*

K. The student will understand and consider the limitations of the collection when planning a research project.

L. The student will be able to plan an efficient search strategy and to complete a comprehensive literature search on a particular topic using library, campus, and other resources as appropriate.

M. The student will be able to evaluate resources, to select the bibliographic citations most relevant to a specific problem, and to distinguish between primary and secondary sources.

N. The student will be able to: a. identify seminal works; b. trace the development of a theory or concept; identify peak and slack periods of interest; c. interpret the influence of different schools of thought on a sociological theory or concept; d. analyze current thinking in light of the historical development of a theory or concept.

O. The student will demonstrate an understanding of the principles and forms of documentation and will use the form recommended in sociology.

P. The student will be able to formulate a viable problem, to synthesize the ideas of others relevant to the problem, to arrive at original conclusions, and to present the results in a cogent, well documented paper.

APPENDIX II

Excerpted from Tusculum College's 1978
"Proposal to the Council on Library Resources
and the National Endowment for the Humanities"

APPROACH 1: LIBRARY ENVIRONMENT

The first approach to the enhancement of education is to create an environment which is intellectually stimulating; an environment which will foster inquiry and will encourage use of resources. A variety of activities will be utilized to achieve this end.

  a. Objectives and Activities

    1) To orient the library to the user;[1] to make the library self-explanatory through:

      a) Well-planned graphics and sign-work. Mr. Clement Allison, Professor of Art, has agreed that this will be a valuable independent project for an art major and one for which the student will receive academic credit.

      b) Point-of-use programs which will be located in close proximity to specific reference works and which will instruct the patron in "how to use" the reference work. The majority of these programs will be in print form. Some may be in a combined audio/print form (audio cassette and printed notebook of illustrations.)

    2) To create course-related displays which will:

      a) Illustrate ideas, events, problems, methods, and cross-disciplinary relationships relevant to specific courses.

      b) Exhibit creative student work. Each display will be initiated by a classroom/library liaison team.

    3) To sponsor special cultural programs, selected for their relevance to current courses, such as:

      a) Poetry reading
      b) Faculty lectures
      c) Author lectures
      d) Educational films
      e) Discussion groups
      f) Fine Arts presentations

    4) To provide increased reference services for faculty and students through:

      a) Scheduled reference hours. We shall schedule a minimum of 52 hours per week of professional reference service, a service that we are currently unable to provide.

      b) Required reference training sessions for library and Instructional Materials Center student assistants and library support staff. The increase in staff will provide the time necessary to develop a reference workshop for library assistants. It is likely that the workshop will include several units that will be scheduled for the first three or four Saturdays of each fall quarter.

      c) Increased library hours. Currently the library is closed on Saturdays. With the increased staff the library will be open on Saturdays and will provide professional reference service.

  b. Evaluation

Student and faculty attitude surveys will be conducted early in the first grant year and periodically throughout the grant period to determine the effect of the improved library environment on user attitudes. Periodic comparison of library use statistics will also be used in the evaluation of this approach. Section IV. C. describes more fully the plans for evaluation.

---

[1] Taylor, Robert S. The Making of a Library. New York: Wiley-Becker-Hayes, 1972, p. 95.

APPROACH 2: LIBRARY/CLASSROOM LIAISONS

One of the rewarding results of this LSEP year has been the enthusiastic response of key faculty to the opportunities for cooperative library/classroom planning to meet specific curricular needs. Library/classroom liaisons have been established for the English, biology, and sociology/social services programs. These will be continued by the present library staff. The desire for similar liaisons with other academic programs has been expressed. The library has been asked to play an active role in the development of materials for a new 12 quarter hour sophomore humanities sequence. (cf. Appendix A.) The Division of Professional Education has indicated specific areas of need which require library staff time and equipment, neither of which is currently available. Our proposed program provides for the establishment of active library/classroom liaisons in these areas during the first grant year, and in the remaining major disciplines by the end of the grant period.

a. Objectives and Activities
1) To institute formal and informal means of communication among classroom and library faculty which will afford an awareness of the information needs of the faculty and students, and knowledge of both established and new library resources and services. This channel of communication will facilitate:
   a) Development of library collections and services based on curricular needs.
   b) Preparation of course-related bibliographies.
   c) Development of class assignments based on available resources.
   d) Identification and development of supplementary materials for courses.
   e) Development of course-related displays and enrichment programs.
   f) Constructive criticism and suggestions for improved library services.
   g) Joint library/classroom responsibility for tutorials and independent studies.
2) To provide for staff development opportunities through:
   a) Faculty workshop on bibliographic instruction.
   b) Faculty visits to successful programs on other campuses; e.g.,
      Sangamon State University's "Instructional Services Librarians"
      Dickinson College's "Research and Discovery in Humanities 101"
      Concord College's "Social Work Issues Seminar, or a Librarian in the Classroom"
      University of Toledo's "Integrated Bibliographic Instruction for Education Students"
   c) Outside consultants.
   d) Librarian's participation in:
      i) LOEX conferences
      ii) SELA/SWLA program "Planning for Effective Orientation and Instruction".

b. Evaluation

Evaluation of the library/classroom liaisons will be accomplished through informal faculty conferences and through a faculty questionnaire. Section IV. C. describes more fully the plans for evaluation.

APPROACH 3: BIBLIOGRAPHIC INSTRUCTION

Every academic discipline has unique information needs, information sources, and bibliographic access routes to those sources. What a student needs to know in order to effectively utilize library resources depends upon his subject and level of need. The aim of the bibliographic instruction approach is to provide all Tusculum College students with this subject search knowledge at the time and level of need. It will involve all Tusculum faculty and will reach all Tusculum students. Classroom and library faculty will work in close collaboration to complete the development and implementation of a comprehensive, sequential program of course-related bibliographic instruction. This approach will be comprehensive inasmuch as it will be established in all major disciplines, and it will be sequential with each level of instruction building upon and reinforcing the preceding levels. When implemented in full it will result in an upgrading of the quality of undergraduate research papers and in better preparation of Tusculum students for graduate work and for continuing self-education. It will also equip Tusculum graduates, as working professionals, to keep abreast of current developments in their respective fields.

The bibliographic instruction approach will include three phases. Phase I will provide instruction for all Tusculum freshmen in the basic information handling skills necessary for a first college-level term paper. Piloted during the LSEP grant year, Phase I will be implemented by the current library staff in all freshmen English classes in the fall of 1978. Phase II will be implemented in a required sophomore humanities sequence. It will provide for both reinforcement and augmentation of the basic library use skills introduced in Phase I. Development and implementation of Phase II is contingent upon an increase in library staff positions. Phase III will prepare juniors and seniors for scholarly research in their major fields of study. Additional staff will be necessary to develop this phase of the bibliographic instruction component in disciplines other than sociology/social services, which were the subjects of the 1977-78 LSEP grant.

The following narrative describes in greater detail each of the three phases of the comprehensive, sequential bibliographic instruction component. Taken individually, each phase is designed to meet the increasingly sophisticated and specialized information needs of students as they progress through their individual programs of study. Taken in toto, the phases form a comprehensive approach which will meet the varied information needs of students in all disciplines.

PHASE I

    a. Overview.

        Phase I, piloted during the LSEP grant year, is designed to equip all freshmen (180-220 students) with the basic research skills necessary to prepare their first college-level term paper. The purpose of Phase I is to acquaint beginning college freshmen with library facilities, organization patterns, circulation procedures, and staff; and to enable them to locate and to use general information sources. This phase will be implemented as an integral part of the required freshman English course (Eng. 102) and will involve the collaboration of the library coordinator and three members of the English faculty.

PROJECT LOEX ANNUAL REPORT

Carolyn A. Kirkendall
Director, LOEX Clearinghouse
Center of Educational Resources
Eastern Michigan University

As most of you represent libraries which are paid LOEX members, this Conference seems a most appropriate time to present a short annual report from our national clearinghouse, which you have so loyally supported.

The LOEX clearinghouse, as most of you know, was established in 1972, operated for three years under grant funding from the Council on Library Resources, and now is a financially self-supporting office. The success which we've enjoyed so far is due directly to your cooperation and support. We continue to carry enough institutional membership/subscription payments and renewals to allow us to staff the LOEX exchange on a half-time basis, and I would like to take this opportunity to convey a grateful thank you to those of you responsible for our continuation.

During the past year, we have catalogued lots of new materials and now have almost 15,000 samples in our collection. We've received about 2,000 requests for information and samples during the past year, we've mailed out some 28 traveling exhibits, circulated over 15,000 separate samples, and have written letters -- excluding answers to the 2,000 requests -- an additional 3,000 times.

The LOEX *News* continues to be issued quarterly, and we would be happy to include notice of your library's instructional activity. Please keep us informed. Within the next year we will begin to conduct another update of membership activity to provide current details.

Similarly, I hope you will also please feel free to respond to the opinion/statements included in the Library Instruction Column of the *JAL*, so that feedback from these comments can also be included in future columns.

It is always interesting to me to view the American world of library and bibliographic instruction from the central vantagepoint of a national clearinghouse, and watch the progress and pitfalls that have occurred.

During the past year, we've received the highest number of requests to borrow the following kinds of samples, and so we can also generalize that these are the areas currently attracting the most attention and effort:

- library skills credit course materials: probably the most universal request received during the past year;

- workbooks in library skills;

- samples of tests to assess students' knowledge of library use -- probably the most timely request we receive;

- samples used in on-line searching -- not just PR materials, but teaching aids and guides: probably the material most urgently needed right now;

- guides to search strategy;

- nuts/and/bolts directions on producing av materials;

- subject-related library skills exercises;

- samples of any letters and communications sent to faculty members;

- library sign system materials.

State clearinghouses continue to be established -- in Hawaii, in Oklahoma, in Florida and in Pennsylvania since January or so of 1979.

Commercial publishers continue to be interested in the great potential market which library instruction represents.

Workshops and seminars -- statewide, regional and national -- continue to be scheduled, as a look at any Coming Events column in the *LOEX News* issues will indicate.

In my opinion, the most telling proof that library and bibliographic instruction is here to stay, at least for a while, is this statistic in literal black and white:

In the early April issues of *American Libraries* and the *C&RL News*, in the Help Wanted sections, every position which includes "reference" or "public service" in the title of the job also includes the requirement of "instruction" or "orientation" or "assists in teaching library use" or similar terminology. Five years ago, not *one* of these job descriptions mentioned this requirement. This tells me that whoever is writing these descriptions, and interviewing job applicants, must also have some sort of program going on at the library, or wish to instigate one, and this to me is very good news.

More evidence, also, that instruction continues to be an important topic in the library world is the thickness of the yellow bibliography, which you all have in your registration packet. Last year's Conference bibliography was 17 pages; this year, Hannelore located relevant citations to cover 21 pages.

One of the major concerns of those in the field today is the whole question of sequential library skills. If there were some way to assure that the entering college student could be familiar with the basics of library use on a kind of standardized level, as sequential math and reading skills are also similarly rated and are uniform, then the job of the academic librarian would be much relieved, a great deal of repetition would be avoided, and time would be provided for bibliographic instruction programs so widely needed. This topic has been and will be addressed at several seminars and conferences this year. It is an issue which requires lots of thinking and work, which will draw a great deal of attention and debate, and one which all of us should be vitally interested in.

One of the major responsibilities of the LOEX clearinghouse is the annual coordination of this Conference. Next year will bring the 10th annual meeting in this series. At this time I would like to announce that the theme for the 10th year will be one of both looking back and of summarizing, and that of predicting the future. It will be called something like Decisions and Directions for the Decade, and we are very much looking forward to preparing for our 10th annual program. What we have already decided is to incorporate something a little different into one part of the program. We are looking for a panel of five volunteer speakers, who will each take 15 minutes, to present their views on a variety of subjects which we will choose, as a kind of devil's advocate. We are not looking in this case for the scholarly, documented presentation, but for five spontaneous, refreshing and, above all, honest comments addressing, for example, the following concerns:

- What are the limitations of library instruction? Where won't it work? Where shouldn't it be used? How truly vital do you think it is?

- Why is it that most instruction librarians seem to be young? Do they wear out? In general is instruction a duty considered appropriate only for the beginning librarian? Why don't job descriptions for library directors include the phrase "must be committed to instruction?"

---- Where are the students -- after this decade of instructional activity in so many academic libraries -- who have benefited from this service? Where is the proof -- if you had to produce some -- that all this effort has been worthwhile?

---- Underneath it all, is it still true that the success of any instruction activity depends 90 percent on the personality of the librarian? Can you prove in 1979/1980 that it does not?

---- It's easy for a small college/university library to have a noticeably good instruction program and reputation; it's impossible for a large research institution to duplicate this record on a widespread basis -- do you agree?

---- If instruction is successful, and others at your institution want to help provide it, and more and more want to receive it, is it true that any good working program will automatically become a monster, and create more and more and more work?

---- What do you see in the future for us? Where and how often (and how widespread) have we failed -- and are we continuing to repeat the same mistakes?

In short, we are looking for some program participants who are willing to speak their minds, not necessarily negatively but to ask these sorts of candid questions, and perhaps provide some answers. We will be issuing a call for papers in library-related journals later in the year, and hope that out there, there are some of you who will be willing to share your opinions without resorting to footnotes and formal rhetoric, but with candor and enthusiasm and spontaneity.

To conclude this report, I urge you to feel free to write to the LOEX office for particulars in any area at any time. We do provide an initial mailing of loan samples or we will dig out answers for your question free-of-charge. Thank you again for your support, and for your friendship.

STRATEGIES FOR PROMOTING
LIBRARY INSTRUCTION

Charles W. Brownson
Reference/Instruction Librarian
Christopher Newport College Library

The question before us at this conference is one of response to curriculum reform. I think there are two ways this question can be approached from a practical or strategic standpoint: either as response to curriculum reforms initiated by others, or as the active promotion of particular reforms.[1] Library instruction is, itself, a curriculum reform. Those who have argued for library instruction at Monteith, Earlham, Sangamon State, Hamline, and elsewhere, have not confined themselves to local benefits, but have argued for a greater educational mission for the college and the society.[2]

The matter of response to changes initiated by others consumes most of our time, but the strategic problems here are chiefly problems of communication: the chief difficulty is to be sure of hearing of proposed changes in time to make preparations for them.[3] It is the promotion of library instruction as a curriculum reform which presents the more interesting problems, and it is on these that I propose to speak.

I want to describe to you some of my experiences in three years of a new library instruction program at a small college, and to try to draw from these experiences some strategic principles which will be of use in promoting library instruction.

Christopher Newport College presents interesting tactical problems to a library instruction program. Communication is sometimes difficult and resources of all sorts are few. CNC is an urban commuter school offering a four-year professional and liberal arts program to about 4,000 students of mixed ages and of mixed vocational and educational goals. Many are part-time; many are poorly prepared; many are non-traditional. About one-third of the faculty are moonlighters borrowed from elsewhere. Campus life is minimal, and the faculty and students are largely inaccessible except at class time. There are problems of resources as well: Christopher Newport College was a branch campus during the fat times and benefited little. The collection is a mere 80,000 volumes after 18 years. There are only four non-administrative librarians. One librarian, with no help, is responsible for the whole of the library instruction program and for all of the reference services.

This is the context in which it was decided to establish a program of library instruction. When I was hired, the decision to offer a credit course in library skills had already been made by the Library Director and the negotiations for this were nearly complete. The negotiations had been carried on through the sympathetic faculty library committee, which meets in the Director's office. There are few organizational barriers to offering a library course: topics courses can be offered without the procedures necessary to formally establish a course in the curriculum, and there are several paper departments on campus through which inter-disciplinary or otherwise unattached courses can be offered. (Paper departments have no separate faculty and therefore generate no separately accountable costs.)

The course has been taught four times in three years, including once by petition. It has generated considerable enthusiasm in the students who have completed it, and every term I receive dozens of inquiries about the course. Yet enrollment in the course has declined, and every term I hear excuses from dozens of students who go out of their way to tell me they would have registered for the course, but didn't.

I want to suggest five hypotheses about innovation in education which I think are applicable to this case, and which may help to explain it and similar cases.[4]

1. The authority for an innovation must come from the top of a bureaucratic organization.[5] This does not mean, of course, that the ideas must originate at the top, or the impetus come from the top exclusively. But once the change to be made has been decided on, however the decision is reached, the authority for the change must come from the top. This is certainly the only practical means of effecting change in library instruction, and it may be the only reliable, successful method. The machinery that was used to establish a credit course in library skills at Christopher Newport College would not have responded to a librarian of instructor rank acting alone.[6]

2. An innovation should not be a status threat.[7] Those which are, are more difficult to implement. Status problems arising from librarians in teaching roles often prevent the establishment of any library instruction program;[8] this sort of problem I wish to set aside in order to pursue a narrower hypothesis. There should be a vacancy in the organizational structure for the proposed innovation: let us speak of

competition for territory, of status threats arising from one's position in the organization rather than from personal role. When a library instruction program is in competition with another part of the curriculum for territory the library, which is a service agency primarily, is likely to find itself the weaker competitor.[9] In the case of Christopher Newport College the vacant territory -- topics courses and paper departments -- was created to prevent faculty imperialism and was later turned to the library's benefit.

Here it would be useful to point out that smaller colleges have a theoretical advantage with regard to bureaucratic authority and territory because, being smaller, the organization is less fragmented, and, being more intimate, communication is freer.

3. Conservative innovations are easier to implement. An innovation perceived as radical or risky will be resisted, and a tactic which attempts to disguise radicalness or to shift the risk is dangerous. A library skills course was readily accepted by the faculty and the students because, in part, it is instruction in its most traditional and easily recognized form.

4. An innovation must have cash value to the persons it is designed to benefit. (The term is William James's.) This is the point made by advocates of course-related instruction. Instruction will not be successful unless the instructed see the need for it, but this point applies as well to the faculty member whose students, it is claimed, will benefit, and the administrator who is asked to spend money to improve instruction. The requirement of cash value applies equally to credit courses, workbooks, and course-related instruction, and the lack of cash value suggests why orientation, consultations, and term paper clinics often fail. If students do not think they need to use the library to get grades good enough to satisfy themselves, then the point of library instruction is dulled and the ability of the library to offer instruction is curtailed or denied. In the case of Christopher Newport College's credit course, I have no reason to believe that the market for it is exhausted. Some in the library and the administration believe the trouble is lack of publicity. (I am investigating both of these possibilities.) I think that the reason that everyone seems interested in the course but no one takes it is that the course is a free elective: it does not contribute to any distribution requirement or major. The course does not have cash value not because its content is useless but because the credits spent on it are almost

wasted. It seems that to the student the cash value is in progress toward the diploma above all. The students admit that library research skills have cash value, but learning the skills is a kind of investment which causes cash flow problems.

5. An innovation must become embedded in the routine structure of the organization if it is to survive.[10] It must, perhaps, cease to be perceived as an innovation. Everyone is familiar with library instruction programs which start strongly and then burn out. In the initial stages everything is accomplished by individual effort, face-to-face negotiation, and the force of personality. The smaller the school the more can be done this way. But bureaucracies are blind to activity which is not embedded in the organizational structure. The result is that an unembedded program has to re-justify itself continuously and eventually self-destructs. Failure to embed a program is usually the result of a lack of bureaucratic authority or an unresolvable battle for territory, but not necessarily. Embedding the library skills course would require an appearance before the curriculum committee. However, our approach to this was leisurely, a battle over the core curriculum intervened, and now declining enrollment makes it unwise to present the course as a regular offering.

There is another element of the library instruction program at Christopher Newport College from which we might learn something about strategy. When the program was a year old a library skills workbook was developed (on the model of the UCLA workbook by Miriam Dudley) with the goal of placing it in the freshman composition program as a required text. I had two purposes: to reach more students earlier in their college careers and to replace the time-consuming special preparations for separate lower-division courses with a less labor-intensive and more systematic method.

After pilot studies the first step was to print fifty workbooks. Some of these were distributed to the college administration and faculty and the rest were put into the college bookstore for consignment sale (none was sold). I kept one salesman's copy, which I bound in soft laminated covers. The workbook was presented to the faculty of the English Department the next fall by the department chair, a person who is an active supporter of the library, at a meeting at which I was not present. The workbook was accepted. From this point the administrative aspects were worked out with the coordinator of the freshman composition program. I have never spoken to the instructors about the workbook except at the invitation of the program coordinator.

The workbook's effectiveness as a method of instruction has exceeded my expectations, and it is the superior of the credit course in its ability to promote library instruction. It is a great advantage to be able to say, as for instance to new faculty at orientation, that you may expect your students to have such and such library skills. (They may not have the skills, of course, but it can be expected of them.) The response of the instructors of freshman composition has been interesting: they resist the uniformity the workbook imposes on them. It is supposed to be a required text but some have made it optional and requested less effective library tours. Others have made it optional in part, customizing it. Yet there seems to be a general awareness of the workbook's benefits and no one has suggested that anything in our way of using it be changed.

Each of the five hypotheses about innovations which I drew from the experience with the library skills course is applicable to the self-paced workbook. The experience with the workbook shows, I think, some of the interactions between these five principles.

The workbook was designed to be self-contained: it is self-paced, self-explanatory, and handled entirely within the library. I anticipated (correctly) that this would increase the attractiveness of the workbook to the faculty by relieving them of potential burdens. I anticipated also (correctly) that a self-contained workbook would be less territorial:[11] it requires no change in teaching style, usurps no teaching time, does not risk exposing an instructor's ignorance of the library, and makes no claims about the other goals of the composition program. The virtues of self-containment, however, make the workbook more difficult to embed: the instructors have so little to do with it that their commitment to it is low and they pay little attention to it. They require to be periodically reminded of it. This will probably always be necessary. Re-education of the instructors about the workbook should itself become embedded, as, for example, through my routine attendance at the department's organizational meeting each fall.

I think we are now in a position to add to the list of prepositions about effective innovation.

6. Effective embedding of innovations requires an effective communication network. The librarian instructor must be plugged into the routine communication pattern of the college. We take it as axiomatic that a 4,000 to 1 student to teacher ratio, as prevails in typical library instruction programs, requires some system and efficiency in instructional method. Conventional instruction methods are too labor-intensive for such situations. So should we take it as

axiomatic that a 200 to 1 faculty to librarian ratio, as in the library instruction program at Christopher Newport College, requires some efficiency in gathering information and keeping informed. Continuous personal effort will not be effective for a job of this size. Going to meetings to keep informed is out of the question: there are too many meetings.[12] Informal networks (grapevines) may be relatively effective on small campuses[13] but the ability to attract informants is a talent unevenly distributed. In any case, grapevines are more unreliable the more important the issue is, and the consequences of being uninformed are very serious. A library instruction program which is unable to respond to changes elsewhere in the institution risks appearing superfluous and in any case, when one lacks membership in a communications network one lacks the means to make a case. One excellent solution to this problem would be for the librarian instructor to become established as part of an instructional development program of the sort designed to improve the teaching abilities of the faculty.[14] Unfortunately, such programs are rare.

7. Every innovation requires an ante from those who will be involved in implementing it. There are two ways of attacking this matter: you can raise the ante and make it harder for those already in the game to drop out, or you can lower the ante and make the game more attractive to new players.[15] Any encouragement of personal involvement and commitment raises the ante; cultivating faculty relationships, the best single promotional method, works this way. In the case of the library skills workbook the ante was lowered: the workbook was packaged and presented to the department as ready to go – in fact, as already in use informally.

Obviously there must be a trade-off here. In the case of the workbook the ante was lowered to the point that the commitment of the instructors to it was reduced, and now that the workbook has been generally accepted a way will have to be found to raise the ante a bit to keep it from being customized too radically.

8. An innovation may have value in itself or as a gate-keeper (or both). Innovations which are gate-keepers make other innovations easier to implement. At Christopher Newport College the credit library skills course, for example, has functioned as a sort of loss leader, lending respectability to the whole program and making other innovations more acceptable. The workbook has gate-keeper virtues as well,

we have found. Gate-keeper innovations are particularly important to small schools with limited resources, which must get maximum value for every investment. It would be nice to be able to predict which innovations will serve as gate-keepers. I suspect, however, that too much depends on the particularly psychological mix of a school and the particular pattern of resistances for much to be done in the way of prediction as yet.

With these eight propositions as tools I want now to examine the matter of course-related instruction, the third major element in the library instruction program of Christopher Newport College.

Course-related instruction is of two types: systematic and on-demand. Systematic course-related instruction (such as that at Earlham, Monteith, or Sangamon State) cannot be instituted just anywhere. The ante is very high throughout the organization and the degree of commitment which is required at the top for so radical a change can be very hard to get, particularly in an institution where there is no particular zeal for good teaching. Any form of course-related instruction poses territorial threats, and systematic course-related instruction requires as much effort to embed as would a new credit course in every department. Systematic course-related instruction has extraordinarily high cash value and high gate-keeper virtues, of course -- these are its chief rationales -- and because of this, if it can once be embedded it is very likely to stay in place as long as there is support from the top. The severity of the obstacles, however, explains why relatively few schools have attempted systematic course-related instruction on any scale.

Course-related instruction on demand (that is, at the request of individual faculty) is the more common form. The instructional virtues of this method are great. But the method also has strategic weaknesses which may make it impossible to realize these benefits.

On-demand instruction appears to the faculty to be a service like reference, appropriate for the desperate; it has no institutional character, no sanction in any tradition other than that of the guest lecturer, and thus it has little legitimacy for those who are dubious about its value. Each instructional contact has to be separately negotiated face to face in a context where the librarian-instructor can rely on his own accrued reputation. On-demand course-related instruction, then, has no bureaucratic authority whatsoever and is impossible to embed. A tradition can be built up with individual faculty, but this is the most that one can expect. A few well-established traditional contacts will certainly improve the grapevine for instruction, but this is a long way from the full instructional partnership that we wish to have. The personal, unbureaucratic qualities of on-demand instruction, however, make it a useful vehicle for promoting library instruction by burrowing from within, as when there is resistance at the top of the organization.[16]

On-demand library instruction is limited to those faculty who make library assignments serious and extensive enough to warrant course-related instruction.[17] Here is the second tactical weakness of on-demand instruction, for within its limited context there is nothing that can be done, without territorial violation, to persuade faculty to require library work of their students. It is a common ploy to get a class into the library on some pretext -- a trivial assignment, or one which the instructor himself views as supplemental to the course. (Some faculty will initiate this sort of thing themselves, saying that they "just want them to know something about the library.") We assume that once they are in the library they can be persuaded to stay, and their instructor can be convinced of the virtues of library instruction.[18] But I suspect that to offer library instruction with insufficient cash value only makes things worse. It makes us appear soft-headed, as if we didn't know the true value of our service.

The number of faculty who give serious library-related assignments may be very small. My estimate for Christopher Newport College, based on an inadequate survey, is that one-fourth or less require any library research whatsoever of their students, and the number requiring extensive use of the library is smaller yet. The market for course-related instruction on some campuses may be tiny indeed, and it is apparent that, if widespread course-related instruction is to be pursued as a goal without the strategic advantages of the systematic approach, then some means of increasing the size of the market will have to be found.[19] This means changing the way the faculty teach, a formidable undertaking. Yet we see in the literature very little but bromides about the necessity of faculty contact.[20]

In the last decade we have put our ideological house in well-enough order, but I do not think that in our grasp of strategy we are yet much beyond advocating personal contacts. I have proposed here eight very elementary strategic principles, but there is another order of generalization above these. Let us do some investigation, and compare the utility of these first-order strategies as they are applied to library instruction programs in many institutions of different types. What second-order strategy might come of this?[21]

For a given situation, which strategies are the most effective? For a given situation, which are the most efficient?[22] What are the common factors in situations that determine effectiveness and efficiency? Do these common factors vary with size of institution, discipline, and so forth, or are they strictly local phenomena and not generalizeable?

I think I could propose more questions of this sort, but this is enough of questions for which I have no answers.

NOTES

1. Knapp (1968). This article is interesting with regard to another aspect of curriculum reform. Knapp, alert and knowledgeable, attempted to predict future reforms. A decade later we see, in this example, the difficulty of prediction and a caution against the finger-in-the-wind method. We need to be hard-wired into the communication network.

2. As in, for example, the papers by Knapp, Breivik, and Farber cited here.

3. Emery, Emond, and Nelson must be recommended in particular as a review of the most important problems and the most relevant literature. See also Dedmon, Farber, and Hardesty. Communication networks are discussed briefly here, p. 7.

4. Most of the principles which I propose can be found in Zaltman. Hardesty's paper is a very useful but much reduced scheme similar to that in Zaltman, expressed in the terminology of psychology rather than that of management.

5. On the bureaucratic nature of higher education see Stroup. Knapp (1964) is an excellent strategy document, extracting from Knapp (1966) the second chapter on the analysis of the structure of Monteith College. Breivik (1978) and also Dillon emphasize the essential involvement of top administrators, in general and in the changes at Sangamon State University. Breivik (1977) in reporting her doctoral research provides an interesting variation on bureaucratic authority not arising from the administrative hierarchy: as a doctoral candidate engaged in research the necessary authority was provided for her by the Department of Educational Services at Brooklyn College (p. 41).

6. As bureaucratic structures proliferate it becomes harder and harder to get bureaucratic authority for a project. Increasing distance between the decision-maker and the person who will implement the decision inhibits the use of bureaucratic authority. This is noted repeatedly by McAnally

and Downs. Supposedly, bureaucratic proliferation affects smaller schools less, but this may be offset by the greater fragility of the smaller bureaucracy: many problems are created, and the number of alternate routes through the bureaucracy reduced, when each office is occupied by only a single person. It should be noted here also that colleges are only partly bureaucratic -- the faculty are organized collegially in part: Stroup (1970). This in itself may cause difficulties, which are multiplied where the library too is organized as a faculty department. Such marriages are often unhappy, and I suspect that the faculty treat the library as bureaucratically organized whether it pretends to be collegial or not.

7. Kazlow concludes that "receptivity to proposed organizational change is innovation specific and a function of organization members' status characteristics and the risks that they perceive as a result of their status occupancy." (p. 96)

8. Knapp (1964, 1966) mentions repeatedly the problems arising at Monteith from dual roles. The necessarily dual allegiance of the instructor-librarian is not always taken into account, but where the two reference groups have very different standards and where, moreover, one of the groups is hierarchical (bureaucratic) and the other collegial, effective work and even sanity may be quite impossible. Knapp (1974) p. 220.

9. Lyle, page 26--7.

10. Breivik (1978) p. 2046, and also Lindgren. Breivik (1977) discusses the subsequent embedding of her doctoral project at Brooklyn College (p. 69--70). Farber, who emphasizes the superior value of personal contacts, also comes around to this matter (p. 75).

11. It is discouragingly difficult to avoid territorial aggression. Despite the low profile of the workbook, in discussions about it with influential instructors I was always in danger of giving offense. In one case I attempted to increase the cash value of the workbook at the expense of a little department territory by suggesting that the department, which is charged with teaching basic writing and research skills, could better defend itself against the inevitable complaints

12. of other faculty about poorly prepared students by putting the workbook to use. This was taken to mean that I felt the department could not discharge its duty without my help.

12. Meetings are also very dangerous, tactically, They easily get out of hand, and the librarian is likely to spend most of the time fielding complaints and explaining why this or that service cannot be provided. It might be best to confine attendance at meetings to those in which the business can be held to safe topics.

13. Interestingly, Emond reports finding no studies of grapevines in libraries.

14. A primer on this subject is Cottam.

15. For example: The counseling center on campus was running some workshops on math anxiety, so I suggested a workshop on library anxiety. I was sure there was such a thing, but had done no research. The idea got nowhere. Library anxiety is not in the canon, it seems. Some effort and research by the counselors would have been required to set up a workshop and to turn the work into professional capital. The ante was too high. I might have been more warmly received if I had done all the preparation beforehand and packaged the proposal, as was done with the workbook, but my qualifications for such research are suspect. It has been my experience that it is impossible to involve a person in a library project with even a very moderate ante unless he is a close friend, or a librarian manqué, or the idea can be made to seem his own.

16. Breivik (1978) p. 2046.

17. Knapp (1966) p. 183. It might be useful for instruction librarians of missionary tendencies to read some of the literature on the usefulness of libraries. Breivik (1977) mentions the problem (p. 12). Harvie Branscomb's *Teaching with books* (Shoe String, 1964) is frequently cited in this regard. The most inclusive statement on the limitations of libraries as information resources may be Patrick Wilson's *Public knowledge, private ignorance* (Greenwood Press, 1977).

18. Lyle, p. 56.

19. Bellardo and Waldhart survey the application of marketing theory to libraries. I have suggested one possibility for increasing the market for instruction: involvement with an instructional development program on campus. Such programs are rare, however, and a library can do nothing to start one. I am currently trying another possibility, about which I know very little as yet: the "assignment alert card." (This idea was borrowed from Virginia Commonwealth University.) The overt rationale of an assignment alert card is obvious: informed of upcoming assignments, the library can prepare in advance. The chief benefits may have nothing to do with instruction – such as preventing periodicals from being sent to the bindery just when they are needed -- but the gate-keeping virtues of removing such annoyances should not be dismissed. The assignment alert card should also improve one-to-one instruction at the reference desk but this benefit seems only theoretical for two reasons: students almost never identify themselves by class and instructor, and it is difficult to get the faculty to explain their assignments in sufficient detail to permit the sort of preparation required by the reference librarian. These may not be insuperable difficulties, but they appear considerable. I suspect they are problems of cash value which might be remedied in time by reports of success, so that faculty and students begin to count on the mechanism of the assignment alert card. Good marketing is essential: the first time, I sent a supply of cards in the mail with a form letter, but it would be better to distribute them personally, say at departmental meetings. The other purpose of the assignment alert is, of course, to identify faculty who are giving, or might be persuaded to give, library assignments appropriate for course-related instruction. Unfortunately, it appears that the overt purposes must be fully realized before the covert purpose will bear fruit: the first responses have been from the familiar core group of library supporters. The market for the assignment alert will have to be increased somehow.

20. Close personal contacts, even friendships, would certainly seem to be a precondition for the change contemplated. But can such a cumbersome, coldly utilitarian strategy be seriously proposed by anyone as a method for promoting library instruction? In this context McGregor's famous theory X and theory Y should be kept in mind. Librarian-instructors may often be guilty of attempting to manipulate the faculty with a set of beliefs much like theory X: most

faculty dislike work and will avoid it if they can; they are self-centered and are indifferent to the needs of the organization; they resist change and above all want security; they are not very bright and are easily misled by demagogues.

21. Librarian-instructors such as Cottam and Breivik seem inclined to disparage the promotional expertise that might be gained from such research. Bothered by the apparent diversity of instructional contexts, they prefer to argue for the personal skills contained in the PhD or the EdD over research on explanatory models.

22. This distinction between effectiveness and efficiency is, I suspect, not made as often as it should be. See Mackenzie for a review of this and other useful matters relating to management research. Small, budget-conscious schools are prone to emphasize efficiency, forgetting that an efficient program is not necessarily effective. Effectiveness relates to ends, efficiency to means.

SOURCES CONSULTED

Bellardo, Trudi, and Thomas J. Waldhart. Marketing products and services in academic libraries. *Libri* 27:181--94 (September 1977).

Breivik, Patricia Senn. *Open admissions and the academic library*. Chicago. American Library Association, 1977.

---------------- . Leadership, management, and the teaching library. *Library Journal* 103:2045--8 (15 October 1978).

Cottam, Keith. An instructional development model for building bibliographic instruction programs. In: *Proceedings of the Southeastern conference on approaches to bibliographic instruction, March 16--17, 1978*. Ed. Cerise Oberman-Soroka. Charleston S.C., College of Charleston, 1978. p. 33--40.

Dedmon, Donald N. A comparison of university and business communication practice. *Journal of Communication* 20:315--22 (September 1970).

Dillon, H.W. Organizing the academic library for instruction. *Journal of Academic Librarianship* 1:4--7 (September 1975).

Emery, Richard. *Staff communication in libraries.* Hamden, CT, Shoe String, 1975.

Emond, Jean. Communication in administration (with reference to the library). *IPLO Quarterly* 14:116–22 (April 1973).

Farber, Evan Ira. Librarian-faculty communication techniques. In: *Proceedings of the Southeastern conference on approaches to bibliographic instruction, March 16–17, 1978.* Ed. Cerise Oberman-Soroka. Charleston, SC, College of Charleston, 1978. p. 71–86.

Hardesty, Larry. Promoting a program of bibliographic instruction. In: *Proceedings of the Southeastern conference on approaches to bibliographic instruction, March 16–17, 1978.* Ed. Cerise Oberman-Soroka. Charleston, SC, College of Charleston, 1978. p. 87–99.

Kazlow, Carole. Faculty receptivity to organizational change: a test of two explanations of resistance to innovation in higher education. *Journal of Research and Development in Education* 10:87–98 (Winter 1977).

Knapp, Patricia B. The methodology and results of the Monteith Pilot Project. *Library Trends* 13:84–102 (July 1964).

────────── . *The Monteith College Library experiment.* Metuchen, NJ, Scarecrow, 1966.

────────── . The library's response to innovation in higher education. *California Librarian* 29:142–49 (April 1968).

────────── . Guidelines for bucking the system. *Drexel Library Quarterly* 7:217–21 (July–October 1974).

Lindgren, Jon. Seeking a useful tradition for a library user instruction in the college library. In: *Progress in educating the library user.* Ed. John Lubans, Jr., New York, R.R. Bowker, 1978. p. 71–91.

Lyle, Guy R. *The president, the professor, and the college library.* New York, H.W. Wilson, 1963.

McAnally, Arthur M., and Robert B. Downs. The changing role of directors of university libraries. *College and Research libraries* 34 (2):103–125 (March 1973). Reprinted in Hug, William E., ed. *Strategies for change in information programs.* NY, Bowker, 1974. p.37–67.

McGregor, Douglas. *The human side of enterprise*. New York, McGraw-Hill, 1960.

Mackenzie, A. Graham. Whither our academic libraries? A partial view of management research. *Journal of Documentation* 32:126–33 (June 1976).

Nelson, Jerold A. Suavity and sacrifice: steps to an improved communication with the faculty in the academic library. *California Librarian* 34:34–44 (April 1973).

Stroup, Herbert. *Bureaucracy in higher education*. New York, Free Press of Glencoe, 1966.

Stroup, Herbert. Bureaucracy in the administration of higher education. In: Knowles, Asa S., ed. *Handbook of college and university administration*. New York, McGraw-Hill, 1970. p. 3–85 to 3–93 (Vol. 1 chap. 7).

Zaltman, Gerald, et al. *Innovations and organizations*. New York, Wiley, 1973.

CURRICULUM AND THE COMMUNITY COLLEGE LIBRARY — PRE-FLECTIONS ON MEETING THE CHALLENGE

Ruth Foley
Director, Learning Resources
St. Clair County Community College

The impact of the back-to-basics renaissance in higher education on libraries in general, I feel, will be moderate. One consequence might be a greater demand for library resources as the result of classroom assignments that force the student to the library. However, the fiscal climate of the last decade has already forced many of us to adopt a strategy of making better use of the resources we have, rather than expanding our collections.

The implications specifically for library instruction are few. Librarians have endured in the last several years an atmosphere of academic permissiveness, relaxation of educational standards, faculty reluctance to provide too much challenge lest students be coaxed to the drop and add lines. The resulting shift away from library use has presented a greater challenge to instructional librarians than the impending shift back to a re-emphasis on general education. In spite of the trends of the last decade, librarians have managed to build library instruction programs and teach library skills to students, perhaps not to the desired degree, yet *increasingly* well. Thus, the reappearance of core curricula provides only a timely opportunity to expand programs that already exist in most academic libraries, and an opportunity to build into those programs the element which has eluded us in the past and left our programs weak — instructor involvement.

While educators continue to debate over what subject matter is essential to a general education, librarians are in agreement that library proficiency is a must. Some librarians have been more successful than others in insuring that library proficiency is provided for through required library courses, although those are few. Some librarians have set up programs utilizing less formal means of instruction — tours, random class visits, self-guided audiovisual tours, and others, as well as varying combinations of these. Regardless of the method used or the skill with which it is administered, library instruction programs need the credibility, the reinforcement that is derived from the integration of classroom and library experience. But students cannot be expected to integrate what the faculty cannot. What library instruction programs need, and have been lacking, is faculty commitment and involvement. Any improvement in the degree of faculty support for library instruction will come as a result of the resourcefulness of competent instructional librarians combined with their effective utilization of institutional governing and advisory bodies.

St. Clair County Community College has made significant strides in the development of its library instruction program. Seven years ago, its skeleton crew offered to English instructors one-hour tours for students enrolled in English 101 classes. Today, a two-semester, five-hour program co-authored by English instructors and librarians, and incorporating systematic classroom assignments is mandatory for every student taking entry-level English courses. Before seven more years, we hope the College faculty and administration will not only endorse the library instruction concept, but will join in the symbiotic association that has developed between English instructors and librarians to achieve mutually beneficial goals.

What librarian-resourcefulness brought this interaction about, and what institutional governing and advisory bodies have been utilized to effect faculty involvement in teaching of life-long library skills? Without minimizing the contribution of our group of faculty supporters, the librarians provided the greatest impetus for the success of the program. Combining research and creativity, they constructed a library instruction proposal to be integrated with classroom instruction, with their objective being teaching students library skills to serve them at the college level and beyond. In retrospect, the library staff identifies these as major elements contributing to the success of the program:

- establishment of a good working relationship with an instructional department that teaches most students enrolled at the College. In so doing, they enlisted the support, over several years, of a large and influential segment of the faculty. Their competence and service-oriented attitude won for them the respect and trust of those faculty.
- recruitment of supporters in various departments -- instructors who had traditionally directed students to the library through classroom assignments -- tactfully demonstrating existing and new resources and ways to use them; informing those instructors of the librarian's goals and suggesting mutually beneficial steps to achieve their respective goals.
- seeking out new faculty to inform them of services and

resources, and attempting to recruit their support.
— conducting faculty in-service sessions and workshops for departments to apprise them of collections germane to their area of specialization.
— serving on College committees and vocal in promoting their program.
— prepare presentations for non-instructional College groups, such as the Administrative Council, the Board of Trustees, to keep them abreast of the program and recruit their support.
— through committee work, frequenting of instructor offices, and involvement in leadership positions in faculty and College-wide associations, attempt to keep informed about courses and activities where one can PR the program or offer suggestions that might in any way bolster the program.
— most importantly – and the element that made all the others work -- demonstrate a willingness to go more than 50 percent of the way to make the program win acceptance.

In combination with their resourcefulness, librarians need to effectively utilize institutional governing and advisory bodies. The library staff and administrator must insist that procedures exist, and are enforced, which will keep them informed of changes in the curriculum that affect their ability to perform effectively. St. Clair's Curriculum Committee data sheet requires a statement from the LRC Director as to availability of support materials from the LRC. Our experience has been that faculty generally do not request such a statement, rationalizing that the new or revised course requires no LRC support, or that current LRC support is sufficient. Historically, student requests for library material do not support the instructors' assumptions, and the librarians' reviews of the collection seldom agree with those of the instructor. Consideration for a student's independent search for information to supplement his study seems lacking in the instructor's assessment of what support the LRC should provide.

At the insistence of the LRC staff, and with the support of Curriculum Committee members, no new or revised course or program proposal can be approved without the required statement. This measure insures that the LRC staff is informed of curriculum changes so that it can consider budgeting implications, initiate action regarding its library instruction program, and make provision for resources in the library to support the change.

In addition to the curriculum committee, a library or learning resources committee can more directly foster the library instruction program. St. Clair's LRC staff will be calling on the Learning

Resources Committee next fall to review its program and carry to the College's Forum -- a faculty, administrative, student advisory body -- a recommendation regarding campus-wide endorsement of the program. And because its members hail from various instructional departments, it is a channel for input and feedback, for achieving that vital faculty support.

The Administrative Council at our institution serves the function of a President's cabinet. Comprised of instructional deans and other key administrators it is an audience for innovative programs. Keeping that body informed about the program gives library representatives an opportunity to recruit the support of people in leadership positions.

The history of our library instruction effort at St. Clair has not been without obstacles. Factors external to the library affect the progress of our efforts. Contract negotiations stifled the operation of all College advisory committees this past year and produced a faculty disposition not at all conducive to cooperative efforts. Librarians have had to work relentlessly to convince instructional faculty that they are competent and have something to contribute to the instruction program, and they still have some convincing to do. The College's structure is such that the Learning Resources Center reports to the Dean of Liberal Arts, yet has responsibility to serve a College-wide function. This structure has made difficult the task of establishing a good working relationship with instructors in the vocational-technical areas where library use has not been traditionally wide-spread, either by faculty or students. Internally, the fiscal factor has provided the most hurdles. Dwindling budgets over the years of increasing LRC commitment to its library instruction activities have forced austerity in some other areas of the library. Librarians, however, can compensate for these obstacles. Some are, by nature, temporary; others will yield to steady, continued pressure. As a remedy for dwindling budgets, consider that more library-proficient students and faculty will result in better use of current resources.

Whether higher education's efforts to reinstate a core curriculum succeed, or merely remain a paper commitment, only to dissipate in preference to old departmental loyalties, libraries will continue to be faced with the challenge of winning the support of teaching faculty if library instruction is to become an integral part of the student's education. The back-to-basics renewal is an opportunity to recruit that support. For this we will need to rely almost entirely upon our own resourcefulness. Now, amidst the debate over a significant educational reform, is an opportunity to reassess our library instruction programs, investigate those of other libraries, and fortified with a strategy, launch a new offensive with vigor.

KEEPING IN STEP BY SETTING PACE

Ann Neville
Instruction/Reference Librarian,
Undergraduate Library
University of Texas at Austin

By its very nature, the learning of library use techniques is different from all the other kinds of learning that take place on an academic campus. The difference, and it is a crucial one, is this:
> No one needs to learn how to use the library for its own sake. For everyone but librarians, the library is not a discipline in itself, but a means to gaining knowledge about something else.

Recognize this, and several ramifications follow. Primary is this: students do not need to learn about using the library in the same ways that they learn about history, or math, or philosophy, or English. Traditional teaching methods are inappropriate and less than effective in teaching library use. By traditional methods I mean separate courses, lectures (mediated or not), exercises, workbooks. I also mean the flashy variation of these methods -- CAI, videotapes, slide shows . . .

All of these, to one extent or another, attempt to teach the student about using the library as if that were an end in itself. Effective library research techniques are always a means to another end. We need to revise the way we think about, the way we implement user education.

Over the past two days we've discussed some of the ways librarians can take advantage of changing curricula. changing methodologies, changing technologies.

Think now about the ways we can initiate change in our own institutions -- substantive change in what students learn, how they learn, and how *well* they learn. Viewing user education as a support to other disciplines makes it clear that we need to show the teaching faculty that, to the extent that they neglect to insure that their students are able to find appropriate information in their own fields, they have failed in reaching their own teaching objectives. To the extent that their courses rely on textbooks, lectures, and assigned readings, and do not require the student to acquire and use information on his own, the teacher is perpetuating the very flaws in the system that are being called into question by parents, students, legislators, and the educators themselves.

Because of the movement toward accountability, toward competency-testing, toward the establishment of goals and objectives for educational programs, because there is a general questioning of the effectiveness of education, we can influence change in the very content of courses in our institutions.

To do that -- and to make it work -- we must begin to think in terms more grandiose than is usual. Instead of thinking about, and working within the limits of "things-as-they-are-now" (e.g., the syllabus of a given course), we need to think in terms of "the-way-things-oughtta-be." We need to learn the goals and objectives of the departments, the hierarchy of skills they aim to teach. We need to know what they think they are doing, and we need to show them how research skills are an important factor that has not yet been adequately dealt with. We need to show them how, by including student research skills as an integral part of the educative process, they can improve the content of their courses and the quality of the students' learning.

In short, we need to be dealing with library user education in terms of its impact on the educative process in general, not merely in terms of pragmatic remedies for pre-existing situations.

We've done enough of prescribing an aspirin for this headache of an assignment, or a band-aid for the use of this tool; enough of prescribing a course of treatment, no matter how extensive, for students' deficiencies in library skills.

We need to stop and think now. Instruction librarians are basically pragmatic, and I think it is appropriate that LOEX, in its tradition of leadership, plans the exploration of the future development of bibliographic instruction for next year. It's time. There are things we have learned, but there are things we still need to learn.

We know that research skills are important for students to have, at least we share an agreement on that. If this is true, then we must accept, as instructional librarians, the responsibility for seeing to it that virtually every student in our institutions has learned the research skills he needs.

To do that, we need to know how teachers teach, and how students learn. We need to work with each academic department to determine the particular kinds of research skills needed in each discipline, and to determine the hierarchy of skills that should be required.

We need to work with individual faculty to develop appropriate course requirements.

We need to teach the faculty what to teach about library research and how.

We need to develop with each teacher the materials to support this instruction.

And we need to avoid the sin of over-kill. All of this does not mean that library research should be in every course in every department on campus.

It *does* mean that we should, when setting our goals and objectives, in planning our programs, recognize the impact we can have on the educative process. We should plan to maximize that impact, and not fritter away our energies on programs that reach only 10 or 20 or 50 percent of our potential audience.

There are not enough of us -- and there never will be -- to reach directly all students at the time they need instruction. But we can reach a high percentage of faculty, and work with those whose courses make research an appropriate component. We can use our time, and our expertise, to teach the teachers.

LIBRARY ORIENTATION AND INSTRUCTION – 1978

Hannelore B. Rader
Coordinator, Education and Psychology Division
Center of Educational Resources
Eastern Michigan University

The following is an annotated bibliography of materials published in 1978 on orienting users to the library and on instructing them in the use of reference and other resources. A few entries have a 1977 publication date and are included because information about them was not available in time for the 1977 review. Also some entries are not annotated because the compiler was unable to secure a copy of the information.

Included in this list are publications on user instruction in all types of libraries and for all types of users, from the lower elementary levels to adults. It was found that the library literature includes many citations from foreign countries on library instruction but only references to items in the English language have been included.

It is again apparent that the interest in and preoccupation with library instruction is growing; the number of entries shows an increase of 30 percent. Thirteen percent of the entries are from non-library journals including the *New York Times* and the *Times Educational Supplement*. Another interesting phenomenon this year is the concern with evaluation of library instruction and with the training of librarians for library instruction. Several articles treat these concerns in detail.

ACADEMIC LIBRARIES

Community College Libraries

Cammack, Floyd. "A Community College Library Instruction System." *Hawaii Library Association Journal* 34 (1977), pp. 11–21.
  A description of the comprehensive library instruction program at Leeward Community College is provided. The development, objectives, operation and future implications of this program

are discussed. The program is based on behavioral objectives, workbook and tests, all of which are part of the English composition course.

Rader, Hannelore B. *Instructing the Community College Library User: The Michigan Experience.* Arlington, VA: ERIC Educational Document Reproduction Service, 1978. ED 152 331. 16 p.

The community college library should not only support instructional services but also satisfy the widely differing information needs of students in the various programs. Library skills instruction would be a most effective way of satisfying these needs. Librarians are advised to develop library instruction programs based on students' needs, objectives, faculty cooperation and program needs. The appendix lists a summary of library instruction programs in the 32 Michigan community college libraries.

Sabol, Cathy. *Librarian in the Classroom.* Arlington, VA: ERIC Educational Document Reproduction Service, 1978. ED 150 985. 11 p.

A description of a librarian's experience as an English teacher teaching the term paper unit in a community college composition course. Various methods for teaching are presented and librarians are encouraged to become involved in classroom teaching.

College and University Libraries

Aluri, Rao. *Library-Use Instruction for Engineering Students.* Arlington, VA: ERIC Educational Document Reproduction Service, 1978. ED 143 367. 11 p.

This paper suggests how librarians can become involved in teaching library skills to engineering students by giving presentations, team-teaching, developing pathfinders and AV materials. Arguments for such library involvement are presented. Also included is a list of 13 hints on conducting a literature search.

Anderson, David L. "Graduate Research in English: A Foreign Point of View." *Literary Research Newsletter* 3 (Winter, 1978), pp. 15–21.

A foreign language instructor compares the teaching of graduate research in English with the teaching of graduate research in foreign languages and advocates closer cooperation between the two.

Antony, Arthur. "An Annotated Bibliography for a Course in Literature and Information Retrieval in Chemistry." *Journal of College Science Teaching* 7 (January, 1978), pp. 163–167.

The author tries to provide an outline of information for chemistry students to be trained in information retrieval. Included in this list are references for general information, science journals, abstracts, indexes and computer searching.

Basker, A.J. "Abusing the Library." *New Universities Quarterly* 32 (Winter, 1977–78), pp. 107–110.

The author discusses the problem of people either getting too much or not enough information. He provides an outline of how to teach library use more efficiently.

Besemer, Susan P. "A User's Guide to Information on AV Materials." *Unabashed Librarian* 28 (1978), p. 29.

The guide is reproduced in full and includes information on citing an AV reference.

Blum, Mark E. and Stephen Spangehl. *Introducing the College Student to Academic Inquiry: An Individualized Course in Library Research Skills.* Arlington, VA: ERIC Educational Document Reproduction Service, 1978. ED 152 315. 35 p.

The course described here teaches students the use of library resources for research. Skills such as critical thinking, research methods and use of library sources are taught and assessed through an individualized approach. Outlines and descriptions of the lectures, practicums and worksheets are included.

Bodien, Carol and Mary K. Smith. *Developing Library Skills: How to Use the University Library*. Report No. 12. Arlington, VA: ERIC Educational Document Reproduction Service, 1978. ED 153 656. 63 p.

This is a text for a one-credit course offered at Bemidji State University and can be used for independent study. It includes sections on the card catalog, bibliographies, government publications, indexes, abstracts and other reference sources.

Breivik, Patricia S. "Leadership, Management and the Teaching Library." *Library Journal* 103 (October 15, 1978), pp. 2045–2048.

Citing examples the author discusses how academic libraries in recent years have become involved in the teaching process on their campuses. Problems which may evolve when an academic library expands its role include staff utilization, faculty-librarian cooperation, new skills for librarians and the role of administration.

Clark, Daphne and Colin Harris. "Can Users Be Instructed By Package?" *Library Association Record* 80 (June, 1978), pp. 279–281.

Explains the library instruction packages developed through the Travelling Workshops Experiment. The use of these packages is discussed in detail and their advantages are outlined.

A Comprehensive Program of User Education for the General Libraries, The University of Texas at Austin. Arlington, VA: ERIC Educational Document Reproduction Service, 1978. ED 148 401.

115 p.

> This document summarizes the comprehensive library user education program developed since 1975 at the University of Texas, Austin.

Dejevsky, Nikolai J. "Introducing New Students to University Libraries." *Solanus* 12 (June, 1977), pp. 1–5.

> The paper discusses library instruction for beginning postgraduate students in Slavonic Studies. Exercises and examinations are also discussed and the importance of faculty-librarian cooperation is stressed.

DeLong, Edward J. *An Evaluative Report of the Richmond College Freshman Library Instruction Program.* Arlington, VA: ERIC Educational Document Reproduction Service, 1978. ED 157 547. 30 p.

> This is an evaluation of a self-instructional library skills program for freshmen at Richmond College. Pre- and post-tests are included.

Dittmar, Jeanne. *Library Service Enhancement Program, F.W. Crumb Memorial Library, State University College, Potsdam, N.Y. Final Report.* Arlington, VA: ERIC Educational Document Reproduction Service, 1978. ED 157 554. 34 p.

> The report discusses the integration of library instruction within established courses in academic departments at the State University College at Potsdam, New York. The project funded by the Council on Library Resources includes the development of guidelines for self-instructional materials and sample outlines for course-related library instruction in chemistry, English and history. A student evaluation questionnaire is appended.

Dubin, Eileen and others. "An In-Depth Analysis of a Term Paper Clinic." *Illinois Libraries* 60 (March, 1978), pp. 324–333.

> This study was conducted at Northern Illinois University. An in-depth discussion of the planning and execution of the term paper clinic is given. The term paper clinic questionnaire is appended.

Dyson, Allan J. *Organizing Undergraduate Library Instruction: The English and American Experience.* Arlington, VA: ERIC Educational Document Reproduction Service, 1978. ED 153 309. 29 p.

> Presented in this paper is information on how to administer library instruction programs for undergraduates in the U.S. and England. A variety of patterns is possible based on findings by the investigator. Commitment to library instruction on the part of the library administration was found to be crucial. Included is a sample job description for a library instruction coordinator.

"Educating the User; New Approaches Tried." *Library Journal* 103

(February 15, 1978), pp. 424–425.
> Summarizes an article on library instruction by L.B. Woods from the University of Rhode Island, some of the recent grant programs sponsored by the Council on Library Resources and some other innovative library instruction programs where librarians are assuming new and different roles.

Eisenbach, Elizabeth. "Bibliographic Instruction from the Other Side of the Desk." *RQ* 17 (Summer, 1978), pp. 312–316.
> A description of the bibliographic instruction course for undergraduates at UCLA. The author documents not only the benefits for the students but for the librarians teaching such a course.

Els, Phyllis M. and Kathleen L. Amen. *Introduction to Bibliography*. Arlington, VA: ERIC Educational Document Reproduction Service, 1978. ED 156 107. 152 p.
> This is a text for a library instruction course at Saint Mary's University. The text consists of course objectives, a course outline, instructional methods and assignments.

Emdad, Ali A. and A.R. Rogers. "Library Use at Pahlavi University." *College and Research Libraries* 39 (November, 1978), pp. 448–455.
> Library use by students and faculty was studied at Pahlavi University, Shiraz, Iran. It was found that library use could be improved especially if faculty would promote it. Recommendations include employment of a full-time reference librarian, development of a library orientation and instruction program and a required library skills course, more faculty-librarian cooperation and more and better library publicity.

Eyman, David H. and Alven C. Nunley, Jr. *The Effectiveness of Library Science 1011 in Teaching Bibliographical Skills*. Arlington, VA: ERIC Educational Document Reproduction Service, 1978. ED 150 962. 30 p.
> This evaluative study assessed whether or not students acquired more library skills through a credit course. It was found that students in the course obtained no advantage in the acquisition of basic bibliographic skills over those not taking the course. Recommendations were made to discontinue the course and to develop more course-related instruction.

Fjallbrant, Nancy and M. Stevenson. *User Education in Libraries*. Hamden, CT: Linnet Books, 1978.
> Provides an introduction to library user education by covering such topics as defining objectives, teaching methods, AV materials production, evaluations, some actual case studies, overviews of user education in various countries, resources and staffing for user education.

Frederick, Ronald D. "Library Orientation." *Improving College and University Teaching* 26 (Summer, 1978), p. 200.
> Deplores library orientation to beginning undergraduates and advocates course-related library instruction tailored to upper level subject areas.

Gwinn, Nancy E. "The Faculty-Library Connection." *Change* 10 (September, 1978), pp. 19–21.
> Explores library instruction through faculty-librarian cooperation by citing examples of institutions where such activities are taking place. These cited samples have mostly been made possible through grants from the Council on Library Resources.

Hardesty, Larry L. *Use of Slide/Tape Presentations in Academic Libraries.* New York: Jeffrey Norton Publishers, Inc., 1978.
> This publication contains an introduction to the problem academic librarians have when faced with the need to instruct large numbers of students and how slide/tape programs could help. Another section summarizes two surveys on slide/tape programs conducted by the author. Two sections summarize how libraries use slide/tape programs for instruction and orientation, data by institution is provided. A section dealing with problems in using slide/tape programs is also included. A bibliography, an index, sample survey forms and sources for further information are appended.

Harrison, Orion. "Projected Methods and the Needs for Library User Instruction." *Assistant Librarian* 71 (1978), pp. 78–80.

Harrison, Orion. *Library Service Enhancement Program. Second Quarterly Progress Report to the Council on Library Resources for the Period December 1, 1977 – February 28, 1978.* Arlington, VA: ERIC Educational Document Reproduction Service, 1978. ED 156 111. 17 p.
> This report discusses faculty-librarian meetings, a student questionnaire which was administered to 4,748 students and course-related library instruction. An earlier report on this grant can be found under ED 148 366.

Herring, James E. "Is Seeing Believing? Library Skills and the Audiovisual Librarian." *Audiovisual Librarian* 44 (1978), pp. 16–19.

Hill, George. "National Package Omits Personal Approach." *Library Association Record* 80 (August, 1978), p. 405.
> This is a short commentary on the pros and cons of using self-instruction packages for library user education.

Hills, P.J. and others. *Evaluation of Tape–Slide Guides for Library Instruction.* London, British Library, Research and Development Dept., 1978.

Howard-Hill, T.H. "Introduction to Graduate Research in English at the University of South Carolina." *Literary Research Newsletter* 3 (Fall, 1978), pp. 151–162.

> The author discusses the English graduate research methods course in detail and explains why he is teaching it a certain way. Assignments and the course outline are described.

Irvine, Betty Jo. "Bibliographic Instruction for Graduate Art History Students." *Art Libraries Journal* 3 (1978), pp. 27–33.

Isaacson, David. "Reaction: The Academic Library in a 'Schooled' Society." *Journal of Academic Librarianship* 4 (March, 1978), p. 27.

> This comment is directed at S. Lindgren's essay in the September, 1977 issue of *JAL*. The commentator argues that librarians can make learning more convivial than teachers and can become very effective in the teaching-learning process.

Ishaq, Mary R. and D.P. Cornick. "Library and Research Consultants (LaRC): A Service for Graduate Students." *RQ* 18 (Winter, 1978), pp. 168–176.

> Describes the formal program of providing individualized research consultations for graduate students through the reference department. An effective advertising campaign, in-depth planning and development of forms and evaluation have made the program successful.

Johnson, Pyke J. "A Day With a College Librarian. Quaker School Library Takes an Activist Role." *Publisher's Weekly* 213 (January 9, 1978), pp. 41–43.

> Describes the activities and services of the Earlham College Library, the required library skills instruction, the active faculty-librarian cooperation and its user-oriented philosophy.

Kirk, Thomas. *The Development of Course-Related Library and Literature Use Instruction in Undergraduate Science Programs.* 4 volumes. Arlington, VA: ERIC Educational Document Reproduction Service, 1978. ED 152 230, ED 152 231, ED 152 232, ED 152 233.

> This project funded by the National Science Foundation had the purpose to help develop course-related library instruction programs for students in undergraduate science programs. Workshops were utilized to train teams of librarians and faculty members from a variety of institutions. Also included are developed materials such as program plans, exercises, evaluations and team reports.

Kirk, Thomas G., Jr. *Library Research Guide to Biology.* Illustrated Search Strategy and Sources. Ann Arbor, MI: Pierian Press, 1978.

> This research guide is an attempt to make available a teaching device for librarians interested in providing library instruction to students of biology. Guidelines on how to use the guide are

provided both for librarians and students. The guide includes chapters on choosing a topic, the card catalog, defining a topic, reviews, *Science Citation Index, Biological Abstracts* and other subject indexes and guides.

Kirkendall, Carolyn. "Library Instruction: A Column of Opinion." *Journal of Academic Librarianship* 4 (March, 1978), pp. 30–31.
>The question of library budget cuts' effects on library instruction is discussed by librarians from Christopher Newport College, University of Kentucky, Cornell University and the University of Waterloo.

Kirkendall, Carolyn. "Library Instruction: A Column of Opinion." *Journal of Academic Librarianship* 4 (May, 1978), pp. 88–89.
>This column addresses the subject of library instruction clearinghouses in the U.S. and elsewhere. Five opinions by librarians from the University of New Hampshire, the University of Michigan, Franklin and Marshall College, Washington State University and the University of Utah are given.

Kirkendall, Carolyn. "Library Instruction: A Column of Opinion." *Journal of Academic Librarianship* 4 (September, 1978), pp. 218–219.
>Librarians from Towson State University, Case Western Reserve University, University of California – Santa Barbara, North Texas State University, Millersville State College and University of Maine provide a variety of definitions of library and bibliographic instruction.

Kirkendall, Carolyn. "Library Instruction: A Column of Opinion." *Journal of Academic Librarianship* 4 (November, 1978), pp. 376–377.
>Presents comments on the pros and cons of point-of-use instruction in libraries from John Jay College of Criminal Justice, Colby Community College, SUNY – Oswego, Monroe Community College, Johns Hopkins University, John Tyler Community College, Elgin Community College, Piedmont Virginia Community College and Pennsylvania State University.

Kirkendall, Carolyn. *Putting Library Instruction In Its Place: In the Library and in the Library School.* Ann Arbor, MI: Pierian Press, 1978.
>These are the papers presented at the Seventh Annual Conference on Library Orientation for Academic Libraries at Eastern Michigan University, May 12–13, 1977. Topics covered include library instruction and administration, the Sangamon State experience, course-related instruction for subject majors, teaching and learning methods for British librarians, library school education for library instruction and new professional directions for librarians.

Kushon, Susan G. and Bernice Wells. *Realistic Library Research Methods: Bibliographical Sources Annotated.* Arlington, VA: ERIC Educational Document Reproduction Service, 1978. ED 143 377. 89 p.
    This guide outlines basic library research methods and summarizes reference sources for government publications, humanities education, history, political science, psychology and Afro-American Studies.

Lavelle, Una. "Engineering Library User Education: The Newcastle Experiment." *An Leabharlann: The Irish Library* 7 (1978) pp. 14–18.

Lester, Linda L. and Lorraine M. Novak. *Directory of Library Instruction Programs in Ohio Academic Libraries.* Arlington, VA: ERIC Educational Document Reproduction Service, 1978. ED 145 862. 14 p.
    This directory summarizes library instruction programs in 18 two-year, 35 four-year and 27 undergraduate/graduate institutions in Ohio.

"Library Instruction: The Right Time and Place." *Journal of Academic Librarianship* 4 (May, 1978), pp. 92–93.
    This picture essay explains the library instruction program at the University of South Carolina library where point-of-use instruction is utilized.

"Library Orientation and Bibliographic Instruction Committee." *Southeastern Libraries* 28 (Spring, 1978), pp. 52–53.
    Gives news about the Committee's activities and summarizes some programs sponsored by the Council on Library Resources Library Service Enhancement grants.

Lynch, Sister M. Dennis. "U.S. by Bus: 5" 'Viewpoints.' *Catholic Library World* 49 (March, 1978), pp. 348–349.
    The column discusses self-paced workbooks and their utilization for academic library instruction.

Lynch, Sister M. Dennis. "U.S. by Bus: 6" 'Viewpoints.' *Catholic Library World* 49 (April, 1978), pp. 400–401.
    This column focuses on problems in library instruction such as AV instruction, faculty attitude, staff problems, administrative support, evaluation and inability of librarians to teach.

Lynch, Sister M. Dennis. "U.S. by Bus: 7" 'Viewpoints.' *Catholic Library World* 49 (May–June, 1978), pp. 451–452.
    The final column by Sister Dennis deals with suggestions for research in the area of bibliographic instruction and for the development of guidelines for library instruction on all levels.

Maeroff, Gene I. "Tests of Minimum Skills Reaching College Level." *New York Times* 26 December 1978, sec. C, p. 5.
    Describes the required basic skills program at the University of

Wisconsin-Parkside which includes required library skills.

Malley, Ian. "Research into Practice in User Education." *Art Libraries Journal* 3 (1978), pp. 17–26.

Manning, Brad A. and Donna M. Buntain. *A Module for Training Library Researchers.* Arlington, VA: ERIC Educational Document Reproduction Service, 1978. ED 145 849. 158 p.

> This self-paced package was developed for people in educational psychology to teach them how to do literature searches. It is possible to adopt the module to other academic areas. The package features units on research skills such as how to do an outline, notecards, finding library sources, using indexes and abstracts, computer searches, organizing and processing collected research materials. Included also are pre- and post-tests.

Martindale, James and Larry Hardesty. *Library Service Enhancement Program, DePauw University. Grant Proposal and Quarterly Reports.* Arlington, VA: ERIC Educational Document Reproduction Service, 1978. ED 145 839. 195 p.

> The Council on Library Resources funded program explored methods to increase library use by college students. Media programs, printed guides and worksheets were developed to teach students library use. Pre- and post-tests which were used to evaluate the program, copies of the developed materials and a faculty questionnaire are included.

Mayes, P.B. "The Readability of Guides to the Literature." *Aslib Proceedings* 30 (March, 1978), pp. 123--126.

> Eight guides to scientific literature for students were tested for readability, e.g., ease of comprehension, using the Dale-Chall, Flesch Reading Ease and Smog Grading methods.

Mertins, Barbara. *Bibliographic Instruction.* Arlington, VA: ERIC Educational Document Reproduction Service, 1978. ED 144 582. 52 p.

> This document reports on library instruction programs in five academic libraries in West Virginia. Media instruction, course-related instruction, and self-paced workbooks are methods described.

Miller, Stuart W. *Library Use Instruction in Selected American Colleges.* Urbana, IL: University of Illinois, Graduate School of Library Science, 1978. Occasional Papers, No. 134.

> The paper provides a description of the development of library instruction and a discussion of 13 current library instruction programs in American colleges. A summary of major factors and problems which emerged from the study is given. The lack of adequate evaluation of these programs is noted.

Morris, Jacquelyn M. and Elizabeth A. Elkins. *Library Searching. Resources and Strategies. With Examples from the Environmental*

Sciences. New York: Jeffrey Norton Publishers, Inc., 1978.
> This guide to research in the environmental sciences provides strategies in finding information in libraries and can be used as a textbook or for independent studies. Chapters included deal with basic library information, topic selection, the card catalog, indexes and abstracts, bibliographies and other reference books. An index and a glossary of library terms are appended.

Morton, Bruce. "For the Record: A Library Instruction Profile Form." *Minnesota Libraries* 25 (Summer, 1978), pp. 311–314.
> This article discusses the need and methods of keeping statistics for library instruction. A library instruction profile form is included.

Olevnik, Peter. "Non-Formalized Point-of-Use Library Instruction: A Survey." *Catholic Library World* 50 (December, 1978), pp. 218–220.
> Reports on a survey of 133 U.S. and Canadian academic libraries to assess the status of non-formalized point-of-use library instruction. Findings indicate that many varieties are used but the printed handout seems to be favored. This type of instruction is a major component of library instruction programs and should be designed with care.

Palandri, Guido. "Beyond Vuturism: Back to Academic Librarianship, 'Overdue.' " *Wilson Library Bulletin* 52 (March, 1978), pp. 568–569.
> Author argues against Robert Vuturo's article on librarians becoming totally involved in the teaching process (*WLB*, May, 1977, pp. 736–740). He feels the librarians' mission is to build collections, interpret them and provide access records to them for users.

Parr, Virginia. "Course-Related Library Instruction for Psychology Students." *Teaching of Psychology* 5 (April, 1978), pp. 101–102.
> Suggests methods to introduce undergraduate psychology students to library materials in psychology and related fields based on experiences at the University of Oregon.

Paterson, Ellen R. "An Assessment of College Student Library Skills." *RQ* 17 (Spring, 1978), pp. 226–229.
> Summarizes a survey of undergraduate and graduate students at SUNY-Cortland to assess their library skills and to compare the level of library skills of selected graduate students to that of selected undergraduate students in biology and health education.

Pikoff, Howard. *Workbook for Library Research in Psychology.* Arlington, VA: ERIC Educational Document Reproduction Service, 1978. ED 151 025. 25 p.
> The workbook was prepared at SUNY Buffalo library to teach

library research in psychology. It includes worksheets and sections on computer searches, dissertations, reference works, research guidelines and other library information.

Proceedings from the Southeastern Conference on Approaches to Bibliographic Instruction Held March 16th and 17th, 1978 at the College of Charleston, S.C. Charleston, SC: College of Charleston, Continuing Education Office, 1978.

Included among the topics are construction of objectives, instructional evaluation, faculty-library communication techniques, grantsmanship and instructional methods.

Rader, Hannelore B. "The Humanizing Function of the College Library or Providing Students with Library Know-How." *Catholic Library World* 49 (February, 1978), pp. 278–281.

Provides reasons for library instruction to undergraduates and gives guidelines and methodology for providing such skills instruction.

Renford, Beverly L. "A Self-Paced Workbook Program for Beginning College Students." *Journal of Academic Librarianship* 4 (September, 1978), pp. 200–203.

The author discusses the use of a workbook program at Pennsylvania State University to teach library skills to the majority of entering students. The program which is conducted through the English Department is based on goals and objectives, features 100 different question sheets to discourage copying and has been evaluated through its two-year use. Also provided are costs and discussions of staff time and involvement.

Roberts, Ann. *A Study of Ten SUNY Campuses Offering an Undergraduate Credit Course in Library Instruction.* New York: SUNY Albany, 1978. 81 p. ED 157 529.

This Council on Library Resources Fellowship Report provides a comparative analysis of undergraduate library instruction credit courses taught by librarians on ten SUNY campuses. Included are summaries of the courses' content, profiles of the librarian-instructors, outlines of various teaching techniques, summaries of interviews with library administrators and academic faculty and a listing of various problems. A prototype of a model course is also given.

Rosenblum, Joseph. "Towards an Alternative to the In-House Tour." *Southeastern Librarian* 28 (Winter, 1978), pp. 235–238.

The article deplores the library orientation tour for a variety of reasons and suggests some alternatives such as a well-planned slide-tape presentation and library instruction based on need and planned with relevant faculty.

Rubin, Richard. "Azariah Smith Root and Library Instruction at Oberlin College." *Journal of Library History* 12 (Summer, 1977),

pp. 250–261.
> The contributions of A.S. Root, Director of Oberlin College Library from 1887–1927 to the development of library instruction in the late 19th and early 20th century is discussed. He distinguished clearly between library instruction and education for librarianship.

Schechter, I. *Library Research Guide for Art History Graduate Students*. MA Theses. East Lansing, MI: Michigan State University, 1978.

Smith, Gerry M. "Cause for Concern." *New Library World* 78 (October, 1977), pp. 189–190.
> The author provides a critical view of library information services, library instruction activities, reference services and recommends current awareness services as a more efficient and cost-effective way of providing the user with information.

Sharma, Ravinda N. "Bibliographic Instruction: Have We Succeeded?" *Indian Librarian* 32 (March, 1978), pp. 166–170.
> Provides descriptions of several U.S. library instruction programs in higher education and stresses the importance of good faculty-librarian cooperation. Compares U.S. library instruction with British user education, the latter seems to be more readily accepted by the faculty.

Spencer, Robert C. "The Teaching Library." *Library Journal* 103 (May 15, 1978), pp. 1021–1024.
> Discusses how the quality of the library and its teaching function is intimately related to the commitment of academic leadership, the quality of faculty and the quality of teaching based on the experience at Sangamon State University in Illinois. Points out some of the unique qualities of academic librarians which make them an important part of the research process.

Spyers-Duran, Peter. *Goals and Objectives of the University Library*. Arlington, VA: ERIC Educational Document Reproduction Service, 1978, ED 148 133. 96 p.
> A report of a program review of the California State University at Long Beach includes among the library-wide goals library instruction.

Stockard, Joan. *A Directory of Bibliographic Instruction Programs in New England Academic Libraries*. Boston, MA: New England Chapter, ACRL, 1978.
> This computer-produced directory lists and describes library instruction in 115 New England academic libraries based on collected questionnaires. Also included is a detailed classified index which consists of an edited computer manipulation of the information recorded in each entry.

Sturges, R.P. "Subject Bibliography in the Service of History." *Library Review* 26 (Summer, 1978), pp. 90–94.

> Library instruction in Danish academic libraries is described. It is organized on three different levels: Courses in library use for beginners, courses in library use to beginning subject majors, advanced courses in library use to subject majors. A detailed description of library instruction to history majors in Odense and Aarhus University is given.

Tanaskovic, Ines W. "User Training as a Component of the Planning and Management of Information Services." *International Forum on Information and Documentation* 3 (1978), pp. 22–24.

Taylor, Jed H. "Research Resources for the College." *Improving College and University Teaching* 26 (Winter, 1978), pp. 89–90.

> Author advocates that librarians in academic libraries ought to become more involved in teaching scholars and students the complexities of information retrieval for research.

Taylor, Peter. "User Education and the Role of Evaluation." *UNESCO Bulletin for Libraries* 32 (Winter, 1978), pp. 235–238.

> The importance of evaluation of library instruction is discussed, principles for evaluation are outlined and problems with existing evaluation efforts are noted. Author offers guidelines for user education evaluation objectives.

Thomson, M. and E.H. Wilkinson. "Learning to Use a University Library Subject Catalogue." *Australian Academic and Research Libraries* 9 (June, 1978), pp. 71–80.

> This is a report of a research study at Macquarie University Library in Australia in 1974–75 to test the effectiveness of teaching the use of the subject catalogue by means of an audio-tutorial combined with a miniature catalogue. The tape-slide program used was favorably evaluated.

Weir, Katherine M. "The Teaching Library." *Geography Map Division Bulletin* 109 (September, 1977), pp. 34–39.

> The paper describes two user education programmes for geography students at SUNY Buffalo. Includes outlines and exercises.

Werking, Richard H. *Lawrence University Library Service Enhancement Program: A Report on the Planning Year.* Arlington, VA: ERIC Educational Document Reproduction Service, 1978. ED 144 476. 102 p.

> The activities generated by a Library Service Enhancement grant from the Council on Library Resources during 1976 are described. Included are a study questionnaire, faculty interviews, student and faculty evaluations of bibliographic presentations and a model library research guide.

"Worksheet on How to Use Resources in Education." *College and*

Research Libraries News No. 9 (October, 1978), pp. 286--287. The worksheet was developed by the ACRL/EBSS Committee on Bibliographic Instruction for Educators and will be useful for librarians who offer instruction in the use of ERIC.

SCHOOL LIBRARIES

Bailey, Barbara M. *Library Charge Desk, Pass Desk and Shelving.* Arlington, VA: ERIC Educational Document Reproduction Service, 1978. ED 152 256 -- ED 152 265.

This is the first of 10 programmed instruction units developed to teach library skills to junior high school students in Dade County Public Schools in Florida. The objective is to train library assistants to work under school librarians. Illustrations, exercises and instructions are provided also for the Dewey Decimal system, the card catalog, magazines, parts of books, reference books and librarianship as a career.

"BL Backs School Project: The Need to Know." *Library Association Record* 80 (March, 1978), p. 128.

This is a description of a one-year program in South Hackney School in England whereby pupils are taught about community information sources to help them with daily problem-solving.

Browning, D.R. *Information Handling in School Project Work.* British Library Research Department Report No. 5343. London: British Library, 1978.

Summarizes a survey of examining boards and schools on library skills for science work in British schools. Though everyone queried thinks it would be desirable to incorporate library skills instruction very little is actually being done on this.

Carpenter, M. "Task Card Instruction." *Ohio Media Spectrum* 30 (January, 1978), pp. 52--54.

Chernik, Suzanne. "Programmed Library Skills Workbooks." *Wisconsin Library Bulletin* 74 (March--April, 1978), p. 94.

The author describes how an adaption of University of Wisconsin-Parkside's Library Skills Workbook is used in Tremper Senior High School.

DuPress, Sherry S. *What You Always Wanted to Know About the Card Catalog But Were Afraid to Ask.* Arlington, VA: ERIC Educational Reproduction Service, 1978. ED 151 026. 49 p.

A description of a library media program for basic library skill teaching is given. Included is a pre-test for 4th--12th graders accompanied by questions for students to test their comprehension. Two teaching methods are suggested.

Hart, Thomas L. *Instruction in Library Media Centers.* Chicago, IL: American Library Association, 1978.

>Provides comprehensive guidelines and suggestions for library skills instruction in school libraries.

Hendricks, B.P. "Student Survival Skills in a High School Library." *South Carolina Librarian* 22 (Spring, 1978), p. 12.

"Individualized Instruction in Elementary School." *South Carolina Librarian* 22 (Spring, 1978), p. 11.

Irving, Anne. "The Art of Painless Extraction." *Times Educational Supplement* 14 July 1978, p. 35.

>The author discusses the importance of teaching library skills to school children and how school librarians should do it, based on a research project under the sponsorship of the British Library Research and Development Department.

Irving, Ann. "Teach Them to Learn: Educating Library Users in Schools." *Education Libraries Bulletin* 21 (1978), pp. 29–39.

Izumo, Patzy M. and others. *Hawaii School Library Media Centers: A Manual for Organization and Services.* Arlington, VA: ERIC Educational Document Reproduction Service, 1978. ED 148 375. 129 p.

>This guide for developing and implementing effective school library service in Hawaii includes a section on library instruction.

King, A.I. "Curriculum Guide for the Library Media Center." *Unabashed Librarian* 26 (1978), pp. 22–25.

Krawchuk, Joan S. "Library Enrichment for the Gifted." *Early Years* 9 (November, 1978), pp. 30–31.

>Describes a library-oriented enrichment program for gifted children in an elementary school in New York. The students discussed even the publishing industry and stereotyping in literature.

Lane, Nancy D. "Introducing Teenagers to Information Services." *Australian Library Journal* 27 (1978), pp. 166–168.

Lasher, E. and J. Hibbs. "Creating a Slide Tape Library Orientation Program." *Ohio Media Spectrum* 30 (January, 1978), pp. 76–77.

Margrabe, Mary. "The Library Media Specialist and Total Curriculum Involvement." *Catholic Library World* 49 (February, 1978), pp. 283–287.

>Six goals are discussed to help librarians in elementary schools who are interested in integrating the Library Media Center into the total school curriculum. These goals are to attract nonusers to the library, to teach library skills using innovative methods, to stimulate gifted students, to turn on the alienated, to become completely involved in the school curriculum and to provide the youngest children with library know-how.

McCarthy, Patricia B. "Inservice at Eisenhower IMC: Helping

Students Help Themselves." *Catholic Library World* 49 (February, 1978), pp. 275-279.
>Discusses a library program for 1,650 students in grades 7-12 at Eisenhower IMC, New Berlin, Wisconsin. Course-related library activities are described.

McLeod, Ann B. "The Harried Librarian." *Clearing House* 52 (September, 1978), pp. 35-36.
>Suggests direct involvement of the school librarian in the teaching learning program of the junior high school by becoming a team teacher, a media programming engineer and a curriculum energizer.

Middleton, Karen P. *Library Skills Instruction in the Fifth and Sixth Grades.* Arlington, VA: ERIC Educational Document Reproduction Service, 1978. ED 157 513. 31 p.
>This is a discussion of teaching location and use skills in the library at the time of need. Use skills include understanding resources, evaluating and summarizing and interpreting information. This should be taught jointly by teachers and librarians.

Rawlinson, S. "Information Retrieval." *School Technology* 11 (1978), pp. 21-23.

Reveal, Arlene H. *Library Instruction and Team Teaching.* Arlington, VA: ERIC Educational Reproduction Service, 1978. ED 144 604. 87 p.
>An investigation of librarian-classroom teacher cooperation to promote library skills in a high school setting is described. Pre- and post-tests and a control group were utilized. It was found that the team-taught group made significantly higher scores than the control group taught only by a classroom teacher. It is recommended that this hypothesis be tried on larger samples. The appendix includes the library skills test.

Scarpellino, A. "Children's Library Games." *Unabashed Librarian* 26 (1978), pp. 27-28.

Shapiro, L.L. *Teaching Yourself in Libraries: A Guide to the High School Media Center and Other Libraries.* New York: H.W. Wilson, 1978.

Tepe, A. "We're Goin to the Library." (Library Skills for Mentally Handicapped Children.) *Ohio Media Spectrum* 30 (January, 1978), pp. 5-51.

Wight, Lillian and A. Grossman. *Maximum Utilization of School Library Resources.* Arlington, VA: ERIC Educational Document Reproduction Service, 1978. ED 154 781. 13 p.
>A full-time teacher librarian position specially funded at Westbrook elementary school in Canada has helped to provide students with library skills instruction and has made the library into a classroom, workshop and research center. It has also

helped to increase the mean scores on subtests of the Standard Reading Achievement Test, Canadian Test of Basic Skills and Library Skills Test of 4th, 5th and 6th graders.

Winkworth, F.V. *User Education in Schools: A Survey of the Literature on Education for Library and Information Use and Schools.* British Library Research Division. Report No. 5391. London: British Library, 1977. 47 p. (50 references.)

Includes British and American materials and discusses the history, objectives, levels, instructional methods, materials and evaluation of library user education in schools. Conclusions and recommendations are provided for further investigation.

SPECIAL LIBRARIES AND GROUPS

"Academic Librarians Teach Library Skills to High School Students." *American Libraries* 9 (April, 1978), p. 200.

The *American Libraries* "Action Exchange" column deals with the question of whether or not some academic libraries provide library instruction to high school students. Five libraries responded.

Evans, A.J. and others. *Education and Training of Users of Scientific and Technical Information: UNISIST Guide for Teachers.* Arlington, VA: ERIC Educational Document Reproduction Service, 1978. ED 146 926. 155 p.

This is a guide for teachers of library skills to users of scientific and technical information in academic institutions or special libraries. Objectives, course outline, teaching methods, evaluations and exercises are provided.

Malley, Ian. "Educating the Special Library User." *Aslib Proceedings* 30 (October–November, 1978), pp. 365–372.

The author provides a definition of library user education and gives a description of the current status of library user education in special libraries. Justification for user education in special libraries is also discussed.

Orna, Elizabeth. "Should We Educate Our Users?" *Aslib Proceedings* 30 (April, 1978), pp. 130–141.

Paper discusses library instruction possibilities for special library users. Differences between these users and users of educational institution libraries are pointed out. Objectives for special library users' needs should concern communication processes between the librarian and user, not teaching them to become self-sufficient in the library. The importance of understanding the organization which the library serves is also discussed.

Parish, David W. "Utilization of a Government Publication Collec-

tion in a Medium Size College Library." *Government Publications Review* 5 (March-April, 1978), pp. 185–188.
> Summarizes evaluative studies of government publications use in the SUNY-Geneseo library. Includes information on the effectiveness of library instruction in the area of government publications.

Smith, J.M. and F.V. Winkworth. *Library User Education: A Bibliography of Teaching Materials for Schools and Colleges of Further Education.* London: British Library. Research and Development Report No. 5436, 1978.

Spencer, K.L. "Legal Research in a Slide Carousel." *Law Library Journal* 71 (February, 1978), pp. 156–157.
> Describes ten slide-tape programs developed at the Law Library SUNY-Buffalo to instruct users in legal reference materials, legal periodicals and indexes.

Wangsgard, Lynda. *A Handbook and Orientation Procedure: Weber County Library, Ogden, Utah.* Arlington, VA: ERIC Educational Document Reproduction Service, 1978. ED 144 605. 115 p.
> This research project describes two methods of orienting library staff members and teaching them library knowledge. One method utilized only an employee handbook, the other method utilized the handbook supplemented by a formal orientation. It was found that the latter method produced superior results. Pre-tests and post-tests which were used plus the handbook are appended.

Williams, Martha E. "Education and Training for On-Line Use of Data Bases." *Journal of Library Automation* 10 (December, 1977), pp. 320–334.
> This article based on a presentation at the EUSIDIC Conference in Graz, Austria in December of 1976, discusses the education and training of users of data bases and on-line services. Included in this discussion are vehicles for education and training tools and techniques for promotion and details on information requirements of the processors, service managers, searchers and users.

ALL LEVELS

Bryon, J.F.W. "The Design of Library Publications." *Art Library Journal* 3 (1978), pp. 28–39.

Cain, Melissa and Nancy Allen. "Library and Bibliographic Instruction." *American Libraries* 9 (March, 1978), pp. 159–160.
> Discusses the library association's response to the increased interest in library instruction in the form of the new ALA Library Instruction Roundtable and the ACRL Bibliographic Instruc-

tion Section.

Corrigan, John T. "Library Instruction." *Catholic Library World* 49 (February, 1978), p. 272.

> This editorial expounds the increasing interest in and concern with library instruction in all types of libraries.

Dyer, Esther. "Formal Library Science Courses on Library Instruction." *Journal of Education for Librarianship* 18 (1978), pp. 359–361.

> The author surveyed 63 accredited library schools in 1976–77 to assess the status of formal library instruction courses in library schools. The summary of the survey is based on 26 received answers.

Hartmann, Jill S. and Robert R. Hartmann. "Inviting Design Helps the User. Any Library Can Have Pleasing Colors and Signs." *Wisconsin Library Bulletin* (July-August, 1977), pp. 161–162.

> Provides some guidelines for pleasing and efficient design in a library to make the library more attractive and helpful for users.

Library Instruction. *A Guide to Programs in Michigan.* Lansing, MI: Michigan Library Association, 1978.

> This directory prepared by the Bibliographic Instruction Committee of the Michigan Library Association summarizes library instruction programs in academic, public and school libraries in Michigan based on information collected via questionnaires. A list of definitions for terms used in library instruction and a subject index are included.

Lubans, John, Jr. *Progress in Educating the Library User.* New York: Bowker, 1978.

> This publication presents an update of the 1974 volume *Educating the Library User.* Contributions by various librarians address library instruction concerns and problems in all types of libraries, school, public, academic and in addition to the U.S. scene Canadian, Scandinavian and British overviews are also featured. A lengthy bibliography and a directory of library instruction clearinghouses are appended.

Malley, Ian. "Library Instruction Materials Bank." *Aslib Proceedings* 30 (July, 1978), pp. 271–276.

> This article describes the British clearinghouse for library instruction materials (like Project LOEX in the U.S.) located at Loughborough University of Technology. The Library Instruction Materials Bank includes materials in printed and media form from university, polytechnic, college, school, public, national and special libraries.

"A Modest Proposal for a Library School Course Dealing with Library Instruction." *Journal of Education for Librarianship* 18

(Winter, 1978), pp. 241-244.

> Gives rationale for library school courses on library instruction and summarizes some surveys of U.S. library schools as to courses on library instruction offered. Guidelines and objectives for such a course are given.

Offerman, Sister Mary Columba. "Let's Make Use of Our Libraries." *The Clearing House* 52 (October, 1978), pp. 61-64.

> Author states reasons for library instruction and provides guidelines for such instruction on all levels from primary grades to college. Also listed are some sources and texts to help librarians interested in teaching library skills.

Ridgeway, Patricia. "Orientation/Instruction Round-Up." *South Carolina Librarian* 28 (Spring, 1978), pp. 11, 36.

> Gives information on Project LOEX, activities of the Southeastern Library Association Library Orientation and Bibliographic Instruction Committee, a new course on library instruction offered at South Carolina College of Librarianship and a program in West Hodges Intermediate School to provide elementary school students with library skills through individualized instruction.

CONFERENCE PARTICIPANTS

Abrams, Leslie E.
Assistant Ref. Librarian
Robert S. Small Library
College of Charleston
Charleston, South Carolina 29401

Anders, Vicki
Instructional Services Librarian
Texas A & M University Library
Texas A & M University
College Station, Texas 77843

Beaubien, Anne K.
Reference Librarian
Harlan Hatcher Graduate Library
University of Michigan
Ann Arbor, Michigan 48109

Birdsall, Douglas
Humanities Librarian
Idaho State University Library
Idaho State University
Pocatello, Idaho 83201

Bhullar, Pushpajit (Goodie)
Coordinator, Library Instruction
Ellis Library
University of Missouri
Columbia, Missouri 65201

Berquam, David L.
Science Subject Specialist

Carlson Library
University of Toledo
2801 W. Bancroft
Toledo, Ohio 43606

Berg, Peter
Reference Librarian
Shipman Library
Adrian College
Adrian, Michigan 49221

Bradley, Josephine B.
Assistant Professor
Sociology/Social Services
Tusculum College
Greeneville, Tennessee 37743

Bradley, Judith I.
Reference Librarian
Assistant to the Director
Mercyhurst College Library
Mercyhurst College
Erie, Pennsylvania 16546

Breitenwischer, Ann
Information Services Librarian
Ferris State College
Big Rapids, Michigan 49307

Brown, Ria
Reference Librarian
Roy O. West Library

De Pauw University
Greencastle, Wisconsin 46135

Carlson, Jolene
Illinois Coordinator/
Reference Assistant
Trinity College Library
Trinity College
Deerfield, Illinois 60015

Brownson, Charles
Ref. & Instruction Librarian
Captain John Smith Library
Christopher Newport College
Newport News, Virginia 23606

Campbell, Anne
Reference Librarian
The Resource Center
Champlain Regional College
900 Riverside Drive
St. Lambert, Quebec J4P 3P2

Cappuzzello, Paul G.
Instruction Librarian
Carlson Library
University of Toledo
Toledo, Ohio 43606

Cevalles, Elena Ester
Ref./Instructional Librarian
Hofstra University Library
Hofstra University
Hempstead, New York 11550

Christopher, Rachel
Reference Librarian
Forsyth Library
Fort Hays State University
Hays, Kansas 67601

Clarkston, Mary Cervantes
Educational Reference Librarian
Trinity University Library
Trinity University

San Antonio, Texas 78284

Cobelens, Mary
Information Services Librarian
Seattle University Library
Seattle University
Seattle, Washington 98122

Court, Pat
Reference Librarian
Karrmann Library
University of Wisconsin –
 Platteville
Platteville, Wisconsin 53818

Crimmins, Mary
Reference Librarian
General Education Library
Northern Illinois University
Dekalb, Illinois 60115

Crowner, Jane
Assigned Reading Librarian
Undergraduate Library
Michigan State University
E. Lansing, Michigan 48824

Dare, Philip N.
Instructional Services Coord.
M.I. King Library
University of Kentucky
Lexington, Kentucky 40506

Dittman, Maria
Ref./Instruction Librarian
Memorial Library
Marquette University
Milwaukee, Wisconsin 53233

Dudley, Mimi
Reference Librarian
College Library
University of California
Los Angeles
Los Angeles, California 90024

Dusenbury, Carolyn
Head, Library Inst. Services
316 Marriott Library
University of Utah
Salt Lake City, Utah 84112

Feinberg, Richard
Assoc. Reference Librarian
Melville Library
SUNY--Stony Brook
Stony Brook, New York 11794

Fidler, Linda M.
Librarian for Readers Services
Conservatory Library
Oberlin College
Oberlin, Ohio 44074

Fleeger, Dale G.
Circulation Librarian
Wilson Library
Anderson College
Anderson, Indiana 46011

Foley, Ruth M.
Director of Learning Resources
St. Clair County Community Coll.
Port Huron, Michigan 48060

Friend, Linda
Reference Librarian
Pattee Library
Pennsylvania State University
University Park, Penn. 16802

Gadsen, Alice H.
Reference Librarian
Walter Clinton Jackson Library
University of North Carolina --
    Greensboro
Greensboro, North Carolina 27412

George, Mary W.
Reference Librarian
Harlan Hatcher Graduate Library
University of Michigan
Ann Arbor, Michigan 48109

Gerdine, Peter C.
Ass't. Acquisitions Librarian
Virginia Polytechnic Institute
Newman Library
Blacksburg, Virginia 24061

Gleason, Sr. Mary Joan
Faculty Services Librarian
Lorette Wilmot Library
Nazareth College of Rochester
Rochester, New York 14610

Hanson, Donna M.
Head, Serial Record Section
Owen Science & Eng. Library
Washington State University
Pullman, Washington 99164

Hardesty, Larry
Head, Reference Department
Roy O. West Library
DePauw University
Greencastle, Indiana 46135

Harnly, Caroline D.
Assistant Science Librarian
Science Library
Miami University
Oxford, Ohio 45056

Hart, James W.
Reference Librarian
Kent Library
Southeast Missouri State Univ.
Cape Girardeau, Missouri 63701

Hart, Sheila
Acting Head, Public Services
Harvard Library
Harvard University
Cambridge, Massachusetts 02138

Haugaard, Anne
Associate Professor
Library Science
Allen Memorial Library
Valley City State College
Valley City, North Dakota 58072

Henricks, Duane E.
Ref./Documents Librarian
Kent Library
Southeast Missouri State Univ.
Cape Girardeau, Missouri 63701

Herndon, Gail A.
Reference Librarian
Main Library
Ohio State University
Columbus, Ohio 43201

Hogan, Sharon A.
Assistant to the Director
Univ. of Michigan Libraries
Ann Arbor, Michigan 48109

Holmes, Christian
Librarian
Learning Resources Center
Bay De Noc Community College
Escanaba, Michigan 49829

Hornbaker, Ann
Assistant Reference Librarian
Main Library
University of Illinois --
  Chicago Circle
Box 8198
Chicago, Illinois 60680

Hughes, Phyllis
Inst. Services Librarian
Hutchins Library
Berea College
Berea, Kentucky 40404

Huston, Mary
Ass't. Undergraduate Librarian
University of Illinois
Urbana, Illinois 61801

Incis, Dace
Technical Services Librarian
Shipman Library
Adrian College
Adrian, Michigan 49221

Johnson, Margery C.
Head, Inst. Material Center
Carlson Library
Clarion State College
Clarion, Pennsylvania 16214

Jordan, Katherine H.
Head, Library Inst. Services
Alexandria Campus
Northern Virginia Comm. Coll.
Alexandria, Virginia 22311

Kasalko, Sally G.
Reference Librarian
Lib. for Medical & Health Sci.
Univ. of Arkansas for Med. Sci.
Little Rock, Arkansas 72201

Kerka, Sandra
Reference Librarian
Undergraduate Library
Ohio State University
Columbus, Ohio 43201

Koor, Judy
Library Instruction Librarian
Bracken Library
Ball State University
Muncie, Indiana 47304

Kupersmith, John
Instructional Services Lib.
Van Pelt Library
University of Pennsylvania
Philadelphia, Pennsylvania 191

LaRose, A.J.
Head, Reference Librarian
Thomas Library
Wittenberg University
Springfield, Ohio 45501

Lam, R. Errol
Reference Librarian
Bowling Green State University
Bowling Green, Ohio 43402

Lay, Barbara B.
Reference Librarian
Undergraduate Library
SUNY/Buffalo
Amherst, New York 14260

Lee, Joann H.
Head, Reader Services
Donnelley Library
Lake Forest College
Lake Forest, Illinois 60045

Lewis, Patricia A.
Ref./Acquisitions Librarian
Rolvaag Memorial Library
St. Olaf College
Northfield, Minnesota 55057

Lincoln, John R.
Reference Librarian
Lakeland Library
Lakeland Community College
Mentor, Ohio 44060

Long, Kathleen J.
Acting Director
Cayuga County Comm. College
Auburn, New York 13021

Markus, Mary Beth
Ass't. Reference Librarian
University of Illinois
Chicago Circle
Box 8198
Chicago, Illinois 60680

Meehan-Black, Elizabeth C.
Reference Librarian
Ogontz Campus Library
Pennsylvania State University
Abington, Pennsylvania 19001

Miller, Elaine N.
Assoc. Reference Librarian
Neilson Library
Smith College
Northampton, Mass. 01063

Minock, Mary F.
Reference Librarian
Lansing Comm. Coll. Library
Lansing Community College
Lansing, Michigan 48105

Mitchell, Marguerite
Reference Librarian
Hugh Stephens Library
Stephens College
Columbia, Missouri 65201

Mitchell, Joan M.
Ref. & Media Service Librarian
Butler County Comm. College
Butler, Pennsylvania 16001

Mogren, Paul A.
Assoc. Instruction Librarian
Marriott Library
University of Utah
Salt Lake City, Utah 84103

Moore, Thomas
Lib. Instruction Coordinator
Bracken Library
Ball State University
Muncie, Indiana 47304

Mowery, Robert L.
Humanities Librarian

Illinois Wesleyan Univ. Library
Illinois Wesleyan University
Bloomington, Illinois 61701

Neville, Ann
Instruction/Ref. Librarian
Undergraduate Library
University of Texas -- Austin
Austin, Texas 78702

Oltman, Jerilyn K.
Instructional Services Librarian
Carl Sandburg College Library
Carl Sandburg College
Galesburg, Illinois 61401

Oltmanns, Gail V.
Ref./Instructional Librarian
Indiana University Undergraduate
Indiana University
Bloomington, Indiana 47401

Pantano, Richard
Reference Librarian
Shapiro Library
New Hampshire College
2500 North River Road
Manchester, New Hampshire 03104

Pastine, Maureen
Undergraduate Librarian
University of Illinois
 at Urbana Champaign
Urbana, Illinois 61801

Pearson, Penny
Head, Undergraduate Library
Sullivart Hall Undergrad Library
Ohio State University
Columbus, Ohio 43210

Person, Roland
Ass't. Director, Undergrad Library
Southern Illinois University
Carbondale, Illinois 72901

Peterson, Billie
Reference Librarian
West Campus Learning Res. Cts.
Ohio State University
Columbus, Ohio 43210

Piatkowski, Helen-Grace
Instructor
Iowa State University Library
Iowa State University
Ames, Iowa 50011

Pillsbury, Penelope D.
Reference Librarian
Bailey Library
University of Vermont
Burlington, Vermont 05405

Rader, Hannelore
Educ./Psych. Coordinator
Center of Educational Resource
Eastern Michigan University
Ypsilanti, Michigan 48197

Rice-Billings, Rosemary
Reference Librarian
Saginaw Valley State Coll. Lib.
Saginaw Valley State College
2250 Pierce Road
University Center, Mich. 48107

Rogers, Sharon J.
Soc. Sci. Subject Specialist
Carlson Library
University of Toledo
Toledo, Ohio 43606

Sandilands, Joan
Head, Inf./Orientation Div.
Main Library
University of British Columbia
2075 Wesbrook Mall
Vancouver, B.C.
CANADA
V6T 1W5

Schildhauer, Carole
Information Services Librarian
Barker Engineering Library
Massachusetts Institute of Tech.
Cambridge, Massachusetts 02139

Schram, Wesley
Librarian
Wayne State University
Detroit, Michigan 48202

Schwartz, Dianne G.
Associate Librarian
Medical Center Library
University of Michigan
Ann Arbor, Michigan 48104

Sharkey, Paulette
Instructional Services Librarian
Arts & Sciences Library
Lansing Community College
Lansing, Michigan 48912

Shenouda, Wagih
Head Reference Librarian
State University of New York
College at Old Westbury
Old Westbury, New York 11568

Shonrock, Diana
Assistant Professor
Iowa State University Library
Iowa State University
Ames, Iowa 50010

Sikora, Judith
Reference Librarian
Alfred C. O'Connell Library
Genesee Community College
Batavia, New York 14020

Skinner, Jane
Reference Librarian
Helmke Library
Indiana U--Purdue U Ft. Wayne
Fort Wayne, Indiana 46805

Snead, Barbara
Head, Technical Services
Hiram College Library
Hiram College
Hiram, Ohio 44234

Snyder, Ellen
Librarian
Wyllie L/LC
University of Wisconsin --
 Parkside
Kenosha, Wisconsin 53141

Soule, Maria J.
Reference Librarian
Library/Learning Center
University of Wisconsin --
 Parkside
Kenosha, Wisconsin 53141

Stiff, Renee
Librarian
James B. Duke Library
Johnson C. Smith University
Charlotte, North Carolina 28216

Stoffle, Carla J.
Interim Ass't. Chancellor
UW--Parkside Lib./Learning Ctr.
University of Wisconsin --
 Parkside
Kenosha, Wisconsin 53141

St. Laurent, Laurie J.
Library Instructor
Frances Carrick Thomas Library
Transylvania University
Lexington, Kentucky 40508

Teo, Elizabeth
Assistant Librarian
Learning Resources Center
Moraine Valley Comm. College

Palos Hills, Illinois 60465

Tiefel, Virginia
Director, Lib. User Education
Ohio State University Libraries
Ohio State University
Columbus, Ohio 43210

Treadway, Cleo
Director, Library Services
Tusculum College
Greeneville, Tennessee 37743

Tyson, John C.
Instruction Librarian
University of Wisconsin
Parkside Lib./Learning Center
University of Wisconsin --
 Parkside
Kenosha, Wisconsin 53406

Van Ess, James
Reference Librarian
Carroll College Library
Carroll College
Waukesah, Wisconsin 53186

Van De Velde, Catherine S.
Reference Librarian
Solomon R. Baker Library
Bentley College
Waltham, Massachusetts 02154

Violette, Judith
Head, Reference Department
Helmke Library
Indiana University -- Purdue
 University at Fort Wayne
Fort Wayne, Indiana 46805

Ward, James E.
Director
Crisman Memorial Library
David Lipscomb College
Nashville, Tennessee 37203

Wayman, Sally G.
Reference Librarian
Pattee Library
Pennsylvania State University
University Park, Penn. 16802

Weaver, Alice O.
Ass't. Reference Librarian
University of Toledo Library
University of Toledo
Toledo, Ohio 43606

Weaver, Connie (Caroline)
Reference Librarian
Strosaker Library
Northwood Institute
Midland, Michigan 48640

Wiggins, Marvin E.
General Reference Librarian
Harold B. Lee Library
Brigham Young University
Provo, Utah 84602

Wilkins, Shirley
Director
James B. Duke Library
Johnson C. Smith University
Charlotte, North Carolina 2821